EFFECTIVE EMOTIONAL INTELLIGENCE

How to Master Self-Development, Relationship Enrichment & Career Success

---

JORDAN REISMAN

Copyright © 2024 Jordan Reisman. All rights reserved.

The content within this book may not be reproduced, duplicated, or transmitted without direct written permission from the author or the publisher.

Under no circumstances will any blame or legal responsibility be held against the publisher, or author, for any damages, reparation, or monetary loss due to the information contained within this book, either directly or indirectly.

Legal Notice:

This book is copyright protected. It is only for personal use. You cannot amend, distribute, sell, use, quote, or paraphrase any part of the content within this book, without the consent of the author or publisher.

Disclaimer Notice:

Please note the information contained within this document is for educational and entertainment purposes only. All effort has been expended to present accurate, up-to-date, reliable, and complete information. No warranties of any kind are declared or implied. Readers acknowledge that the author is not engaged in the rendering of legal, financial, medical, or professional advice. The content within this book has been derived from various sources. Please consult a licensed professional before attempting any techniques outlined in this book.

By reading this document, the reader agrees that under no circumstances is the author responsible for any losses, direct or indirect, that are incurred as a result of the use of the information contained within this document, including, but not limited to, errors, omissions, or inaccuracies.

For Dad

Contents

Introduction 7

Section 1:
Emotional Intelligence & Me
1. Understanding Emotional Intelligence 13
2. Emotional Intelligence & Mental Well-being ... 31
3. Emotional Intelligence in Motion 43

Section 2:
Emotional Intelligence & Relationships
4. Emotional Intelligence in Personal Relationships ... 59
5. Emotional Intelligence in Parenting 85
6. Emotional Intelligence & Culture 97
7. Emotional Intelligence & Technology 107

Section 3:
Emotional Intelligence in the Workplace
8. Emotional Intelligence & Career Development ... 125
9. Emotional Intelligence & Leadership 133

Section 4:
The Value of Emotional Intelligence
10. Emotional Intelligence & True Wealth 149

Conclusion 163
References 167

Introduction

Have you ever been in a heated conversation that spiraled out of control, leaving you bewildered and wondering how things could have been different? Picture a recent disagreement that escalated unnecessarily. It could be with your spouse over something as trivial as household chores or with a colleague about a project deadline. Imagine if that conversation had been approached with higher emotional intelligence (EI). The misunderstanding might have been resolved quickly or even avoided entirely.

EI is the invisible conductor of our interpersonal relationships, the backbone of our online and offline interactions. It influences how we manage our emotions, navigate social complexities, and make personal decisions that achieve positive results. From parenting to leading a team and maintaining friendships to engaging with strangers in the digital world, EI is a fundamental skill that enriches every aspect of our lives.

In "Effective Emotional Intelligence: How to Master Self-Development, Relationship Enrichment & Career Success," I invite you to explore the multifaceted role of EI in enhancing your personal and professional life. This book is structured to guide you through understanding your emotional mechanisms, applying EI in your relationships, and developing EI in your career. Each chapter is packed with actionable advice, practical exercises, and sharp analyses that will equip you with the tools to improve your emotional skills.

What sets this book apart is its holistic approach, combining the latest research with relatable anecdotes and a wide range of practical exercises. It is tailored to address readers from all walks of life—whether you are a parent seeking to connect better with your children, a leader aiming to cultivate a more empathetic workplace, or simply someone who wishes to have deeper, more meaningful interactions in your daily life.

As we embark on this journey, remember that enhancing your EI transforms how you experience and interact with the world. It's about bringing EI home into every conversation, every challenge, and every relationship.

I warmly invite you to embark on this journey with me, to learn about EI, and to live it. By integrating these principles into your life, you'll see firsthand how powerful a tool EI can be—opening doors to stronger relationships, heightened self-awareness, and greater overall satisfaction.

Let's begin this transformative exploration together and unlock the potential of every interaction to be more understanding, rewarding, and connected. Welcome to a new chapter in your life, one filled with emotional clarity and connectivity.

Section 1:

EMOTIONAL INTELLIGENCE & ME

ONE

Understanding Emotional Intelligence

Have you ever been accused of reading too much into a situation or, conversely, completely missing the emotional cues that everyone else seemed to pick up on? We've all been there—one way or another—finding ourselves floundering in the social seas without our emotional compasses. This is where emotional intelligence (EI) is our trusty navigator to help us understand and manage our emotional currents wisely.

EI is often tossed around like a hot potato in personal and professional growth conversations. But what does it mean? Is it a trendy buzzword that will soon be forgotten, or does it hold the key to unlocking deeper interpersonal connections and personal satisfaction? Let's unpack this concept, exploring its scientific roots, historical journey, and the fundamental components that make it an indispensable part of our daily interactions.

The Science of Emotional Intelligence: Beyond the Buzzword

Defining Emotional Intelligence

EI, at its core, refers to the ability to identify, understand, and manage our own emotions and the emotions of others. As Daniel Goleman, a prominent psychologist, and author who popularized the concept of emotional intelligence, puts it, "Emotional intelligence is the ability to monitor one's own and other feelings and emotions, to discriminate among them and to use this information to guide one's thinking and actions." It's a pivotal skill that allows us to navigate the social complexities of the world, adapt to change, and solve problems. The term might sound modern, but its concepts are as ancient as any philosophical discourse about human emotion. Over the years, EI has evolved from a mere psychological theory to a crucial skill set in various domains of life, including leadership, education, and relationship management.

Neurological Underpinnings

Complex neurological activities govern the fascinating interplay between our emotions and cognitive processes. The limbic system, the part of the brain responsible for emotional processing, is primarily profoundly intertwined with the neocortex, where higher thinking occurs. This relationship explains why our emotions can powerfully influence our reasoning and decision-making processes—sometimes leading us astray, other times guiding us towards wiser choices.

Neuroscience has shown that emotional responses are not just passing states but integral to our brain's architecture. When we develop EI, we train our brains to regulate and interpret this intricate dance between emotion and cognition.

Historical Perspectives

The history of EI began long before it was formally defined. Philosophers like Aristotle spoke of managing emotions to achieve true happiness and virtue. However, in the 20th century, EI gained significant scientific attention. In the 1990s, researchers John Mayer and Peter Salovey introduced a formal theory of EI, describing it as a subset of social intelligence that involves the ability to monitor one's own and other's feelings and emotions, to discriminate among them, and to use this information to guide one's thinking and actions. (Mayer, 2006, 172–188)

This groundwork paved the way for Daniel Goleman to popularize the concept with his 1995 book "Emotional Intelligence," which linked EI to everything from professional success to personal well-being.

The Five Components

Goleman's EI framework lays out a series of competencies and skills that can both drive leadership performance and improve the quality of personal relationships. It has transformed the way we perceive and value our emotional capacities in the personal and professional world.

Goleman's model contains five key components that anyone looking to improve their EI should understand and cultivate:

1. Self-awareness: Recognizing one's own emotions and their effects.
2. Self-regulation: Managing or redirecting disruptive emotions and impulses and adapting to changing circumstances.
3. Motivation: Harnessing emotions to pursue goals with energy and persistence.
4. Empathy: Considering other people's feelings, especially when making decisions.
5. Social skills: Managing relationships to move people in the desired direction, whether leading, negotiating, or working as part of a team.

Each of these components builds on the others, providing a comprehensive toolkit for understanding and navigating the emotional aspects of our lives. As we delve deeper into each element in the following sections, consider how each area resonates with your personal experiences and where you have room for growth.

For those curious about where they stand on the EI spectrum, consider measuring your level of EI with tools like *The Personality Lab (https://bit.ly/3w8s4Hg)*. This assessment evaluates emotional perception, understanding, and management, offering insights that can guide your efforts to enhance your EI. It's like getting a fitness assessment before starting a workout regimen; it provides a growth baseline.

By breaking down the science and development of EI, we can see it as a buzzword and a powerful, tangible tool for enhancing our personal and professional lives. As we explore these fundamentals, you'll discover practical ways to apply EI in everyday interactions, leading to deeper connections and more satisfying outcomes.

Self-awareness: The Core of EI

Let's chat about *self-awareness*. Imagine *self-awareness* as the lens through which you see yourself and the world around you. It's like having an internal mirror that reflects your feelings, drives, and desires, allowing you to navigate life with a clearer understanding of why you react the way you do in various situations. This clarity is crucial for personal growth and how we interact with others at home, in the workplace, or in any social setting.

Understanding *self-awareness* within the context of EI means recognizing when you're feeling a certain way and understanding why. It's about connecting the dots between your feelings, the thoughts they trigger, and your subsequent actions. For instance, you might notice your heart racing, and you feel frustrated when running late for an important meeting. Recognizing these feelings and their triggers helps you manage them more effectively, ensuring they don't lead you to act rashly, like speeding through traffic or snapping at a colleague.

So, how does one enhance this *self-awareness*? There are several practical techniques that you can start implementing right away. Journaling, for example, is a fantastic tool. It is a repository for your thoughts and feelings, allowing you to express yourself freely and reflect on your emotional experiences. This practice helps solidify your observations and insights about your emotional patterns. Let's return to the scenario where you are running late for a meeting. Reflective journaling can help you identify the sequence of your emotional response and lead to a realization that punctuality is a value you hold dear, informing your emotional reaction to being late.

The power of reflection cannot be overstated when it comes to enhancing self-understanding. Regularly thinking deeply about your feelings, why you experienced them, and how you handled various situations can be enlightening. It's about asking yourself, "Why did I react that way?" or "What could I do differently next time?" This kind of reflection turns everyday experiences into valuable learning opportunities, gradually increasing your emotional agility.

Another powerful technique is mindfulness, which involves paying full attention to the present moment without judgment. Mindfulness is about noticing where you are, what you're doing, and how you feel right then and there. This could mean feeling the steering wheel under your hands as you drive, noticing the tension in your shoulders when you're stressed, or simply observing the flavor of your coffee as you take a morning sip. Mindfulness strengthens your ability to recognize your emotions as they arise, allowing you to manage them proactively rather than reactively.

Recognizing and naming your emotions as they occur is another crucial technique in developing strong *self-awareness*. This might sound simpler than it is; emotions can be complex and fleeting. However, putting a name to what you feel—anger, joy, frustration, or disappointment—can give you a sense of control and make the emotion more manageable. It's like taming a wild beast by knowing its name. By practicing this, you begin to discern even the subtle nuances of your emotional landscape, which is invaluable in managing personal and professional interactions more effectively.

By fostering greater *self-awareness*, you equip yourself with the tools to respond to life's challenges with calm clarity and a proactive, rather than reactive, approach. Suppose you're dealing with a stubborn teenager, a demanding boss, or navigating your aspirations. Understanding your emotions and how they influence your actions can transform your interactions and lead to more fulfilling relationships and professional success.

Self-regulation: Techniques for Emotional Mastery

Imagine you're in the middle of a heated debate at work or a family dinner, and the conversation veers into sensitive territory. Your initial instinct is to react impulsively, with a sharp retort, or shut down the discussion altogether. This is where *self-regulation*, a pivotal aspect of EI, plays a crucial role. It's about taking a deep breath and choosing to respond rather than react, maintaining your composure, and handling the situation with wisdom.

Self-regulation refers to our ability to manage our emotions and behaviors by the demands of the situation. It involves being conscious of our feelings, assessing whether our default response is the most constructive option, and adjusting accordingly. Think of *self-regulation* as the calm, wise voice in your head that suggests taking a few slow breaths when you're on the verge of a knee-jerk reaction that you might regret later. It supports striving for a balanced response and is also about adjusting your long-term emotional habits for better personal and relational outcomes.

Managing impulses is a significant part of *self-regulation*. We live in a world of instant gratification, where the temptation to give in to immediate desires can often lead us astray from our long-term goals. *Self-regulation* might play out when you resist the urge to splurge on a luxury item for the sake of a goal or choose a difficult conversation with a calm demeanor rather than avoiding it. Managing impulses requires a conscious effort. Techniques like setting clear goals, reminding yourself of the bigger picture, and creating an environment that reduces temptations can be incredibly effective. For instance, if you know you're prone to spend frivolously, leaving your credit card at home when shopping can be a simple yet effective strategy to curb impulsive buying.

Handling stress and anxiety is another critical area where *self-regulation* can make a substantial difference. Stress is an inevitable part of life, but how we manage it can vary dramatically from one person to another. Techniques such as deep breathing, progressive muscle relaxation, and mindful meditation have been scientifically proven to help regulate emotional responses and reduce stress and anxiety. Deep breathing, for instance, helps slow down an overactive nervous system and can bring a sense of calm, making it easier to think clearly and respond more effectively to stress. Progressive muscle relaxation, where you systematically tense and then relax different muscle groups, can also help alleviate the physical tension that often accompanies stress. (Cowell, 2018, 531–533)

Adapting to change is one of the most challenging aspects of *self-regulation*. Change is constant and often uncomfortable, pushing us out of our familiar routines and forcing us to adjust to new realities. A sudden job change, moving to a new city, or adjusting to life as new parents can stir a host of emotions, from excitement to fear. *Self-regulation* helps us manage these emotions effectively, enabling us to approach change flexibly and resiliently. It encourages us to view change as an opportunity for growth and learning rather than a threat to our stability.

In daily life, *self-regulation* manifests in various ways. Consider a scenario where a colleague criticizes you in front of others. An unregulated response might involve snapping back defensively or brooding silently, neither of which is likely to resolve the situation effectively. Instead, *self-regulation* might lead you to acknowledge your emotions, perhaps admitting to yourself that the criticism hurts but choosing to respond in a way that maintains your dignity and seeks to clarify or rectify the situation constructively.

Lastly, *self-regulation* doesn't mean suppressing your emotions or pretending they don't exist; it's about acknowledging your feelings and choosing how to express them in ways that align with your values and goals. This skill supports your development into a more composed, thoughtful, and respected individual in every arena.

Motivation and Emotional Intelligence: Fueling Personal Growth

Moving on to *motivation*, that inner engine that pushes us to wake up every morning and chase our dreams or sometimes to get out of bed and make coffee. In EI, understanding and harnessing *motivation* is like having the best personal coach embedded in your psyche, nudging you toward your goals. There are two types of *motivation*: intrinsic and extrinsic. Intrinsic *motivation* comes from within you, driven by personal satisfaction or the joy of doing something. For example, you might be intrinsically motivated to paint because it feels like unleashing your inner Picasso, even if no one sees your artwork. Extrinsic *motivation*, on the other hand, is fueled by external rewards. This could be working overtime to earn that end-of-year bonus or studying hard to receive peer accolades.

Understanding these two types of *motivation* and how they interact with your EI can significantly influence how you set and achieve your goals. *Self-awareness* is also helpful here. Inward reflection might help you recognize which type of *motivation* drives your actions. Are you staying late at work because you're passionate about the project, or are you more motivated by how it will look on your following performance review? This awareness is crucial because it aligns your goals with your true motivators, making them feel less like a mountain to climb and more like a natural path forward.

EI acts as a spotlight and steering wheel when setting and achieving goals. It illuminates your deepest values and desires (spotlight) and helps you navigate towards them in the most EI way possible (steering wheel). Say, for instance, you aim to become a better public speaker. EI guides you through setting realistic milestones, like joining a local public speaking group, rather than just setting a nebulous goal of "becoming more confident." *Motivation* also steadies you through the ups and downs, helping you manage the inevitable anxiety and boosting your resilience after a less-than-perfect speech, providing you with the persistence needed to navigate challenges.

Procrastination, the archnemesis of productivity, often has emotional roots. Emotions drive us to avoid tasks that we find daunting or unpleasant. *Motivation* can counteract procrastination by helping individuals understand the emotional barriers underlying their avoidance behaviors. This enables them to address fears, doubts, or anxieties contributing to procrastination and take proactive steps toward task completion.

Identifying personal emotional triggers is also essential in the context of *motivation*. Through self-observation and reflection, you can start to notice patterns that motivate or demotivate you. You may be more productive in a quiet, organized space, or perhaps deadlines spur you into action rather than slow you down. Recognizing these triggers allows you to create an environment that maximizes your *motivational* strengths while minimizing the impact of your demotivators. Suppose internal desires or external rewards drive you. In that case, a robust emotional toolkit clarifies what truly motivates you and equips you with the strategies to keep the fires of *motivation* burning, even under the rainiest circumstances.

Empathy: Understanding Beyond Words

Empathy is another critical component of EI. It's that warm blanket of understanding you throw around someone when they're having a tough day. *Empathy* isn't about feeling sorry for someone; it's how you connect with others.

Empathy involves understanding others' feelings and perspectives and using that understanding to guide your actions. Think of *empathy* as the emotional glue that holds human connections together. *Empathy* is helpful in better understanding your partner's frustrations, being a supportive parent, or a leader who truly connects with their team. *Empathy* allows you to navigate the complexities of human emotions with grace and effectiveness.

There are several flavors of *empathy*, each serving a unique purpose. Cognitive *empathy*, for example, is about intellectually understanding someone else's perspective or mental state. Imagine a detective piecing together clues about why someone might feel a certain way based on their circumstances without necessarily feeling those emotions yourself. This type of *empathy* is invaluable in the workplace, where understanding a colleague's point of view can lead to more effective communication and problem-solving.

On the other hand, emotional *empathy* is about physically feeling what another person feels as if their emotions were contagious. This can be both a superpower and a kryptonite; it allows you to connect deeply with others, but without proper regulation, it can lead you to take on too much of someone else's emotional state.

In the dance of daily interactions, *empathy* enriches your steps, allowing you to move in sync with others. It helps you pause and consider your words when you're about to give feedback, ensuring you're constructive without being hurtful. It also prompts you to reach out to a friend going through a rough patch, even when they haven't asked for help, because you can sense they need support.

One of the most effective methods for cultivating *empathy* is through active listening. This isn't just nodding while someone talks; it's about fully engaging with them, absorbing their words without planning your response in the back of your mind. Imagine you're a sculptor, and the person speaking gives you the clay of their thoughts and emotions. Active listening allows you to mold that clay accurately without leaving your fingerprints all over it.

Another powerful practice is perspective-taking. This involves deliberately putting yourself in someone else's shoes. For instance, consider what might happen in your life before reacting in anger towards someone who has snapped at you. Maybe they just received some bad news, or they're under a lot of stress. Understanding these factors can change your reaction from one of retaliation to one of compassion.

Incorporating daily reflection practices can also enhance your *empathy*. Each evening, spend a few minutes reflecting on your interactions throughout the day. Think about moments where you felt a strong connection with someone or perhaps a time when you misread a situation. What were the cues? What could you have understood better? This habit improves your ability to empathize and deepens your overall *self-awareness*.

Seeking and utilizing feedback is also crucial in the development of *empathy*. Ask people close to you how they feel about your interactions. Are you coming across as genuine? Do they feel heard and understood? This feedback can provide valuable insights into how well you apply your empathetic skills and where you might need to adjust.

Indeed, mindfulness plays a significant role in developing *empathy*. Practicing mindfulness enhances your ability to be present in the moment, which is essential for *empathy*. It allows you to be fully engaged in interactions, not distracted by your preoccupations or judgments. This presence can make all the difference in how you relate to others, ensuring that your *empathy* is practical. By weaving *empathy* into the fabric of your daily life, you're not just improving your relationships—you're actively participating in a more compassionate world.

Social Skills and Emotional Intelligence

Let's dive into the world of *social skills* and emotional intelligence, where understanding and connecting with others play a key role. Imagine *social skills* as your secret weapon, helping you weave through relationships and social situations with finesse and *empathy*. According to the emotional intelligence guru Daniel Goleman, having strong *social skills* is like having a secret weapon for leadership and overall emotional intelligence success.

Why Social Skills Matter

So, what's the big deal about *social skills*, you ask? Well, they're like the secret sauce that makes interactions smoother, relationships stronger, and teamwork more effective. Think about it – being able to communicate clearly, resolve conflicts like a pro, influence others positively, and work seamlessly in a team are all part of the *social skills* package. These skills not only help you build and nurture meaningful connections but also empower you to express yourself, collaborate, and achieve shared goals. Who wouldn't want that kind of magic in their social toolkit?

Let's Break It Down

In Goleman's world of emotional intelligence, *social skills* come in different flavors:

1. Communication: Ever found yourself nodding along while someone talks without really listening? Effective communication is about speaking your

truth, actively listening, and showing empathy. It's the art of sharing ideas clearly while fostering open and respectful dialogue that bridges understanding.
2. Conflict Resolution: Picture this – turning a heated argument into a constructive discussion where everyone walks away feeling heard and respected. That's the power of mastering conflict resolution. It's about finding common ground, diplomatically handling disagreements, and finding win-win solutions that keep relationships healthy.
3. Influence: Ever had that friend who can convince you to join a spontaneous adventure with just a smile? Socially skilled individuals have a knack for inspiring, motivating, and persuading others positively. Building trust, credibility, and strong relationships are their secret weapons for driving positive outcomes.
4. Teamwork: Imagine working on a project where everyone's ideas are valued, and collaboration feels like a well-rehearsed dance. That's the beauty of teamwork – blending diverse perspectives, communicating openly, and contributing to group efforts while fostering unity and camaraderie within the team.

Sharpening Your Social Skills

Enhancing your *social skills* is like flexing a muscle – it takes *self-awareness*, *empathy*, and practice. By tuning into your emotions and how they shape your interactions, you can boost your *empathy* and perspective-taking abilities. Engaging in activities that promote teamwork, communication, and conflict resolution can be your training ground for mastering those *social skills* over time.

Remember, *social skills* are your ticket to navigating the twists and turns of social life, building solid relationships, and unlocking success in various aspects of your journey. So, buckle up and let your *social skills* shine bright!

TWO

Emotional Intelligence & Mental Well-being

This chapter will explore how developing your emotional intelligence skills can enhance your mood on a gloomy day and overall mental health. So, grab your favorite cup of tea, get comfy, and dive into the soothing waters of EI.

Emotional Intelligence as a Path to Improved Mental Health

Imagine mental health as a garden. Just as a garden requires regular tending—watering, weeding, and sunlight—so does your mental landscape. EI is like the gardening tools that help you nurture this space, ensuring it flourishes. The link between EI and mental health is robust, with numerous studies affirming that higher levels of EI correlate with better mental well-being. One such study surveyed health workers in Kosovo, who showed that having a higher degree of EI can act as protection against mental illness. (Shahini, 2023)

Recognizing and managing your emotions effectively plays a pivotal role in this process. Think about the last time you felt a rush of anger or a wave of sadness. These emotions, while entirely natural, can lead to stress, anxiety, and depression if not managed properly. By tuning into your emotional state through *self-awareness*—a core component of EI—you can identify your feelings and why. This awareness allows you to address emotions before they become overwhelming, preventing them from laying down roots and sprouting weeds in your mental garden.

Now, let's talk about EI in therapy. Therapeutic settings can significantly benefit from the integration of EI principles. Therapists often work to enhance their clients' EI, helping them to understand better and manage their feelings, which, in turn, facilitates a more effective therapeutic process. For example, a therapist might help you develop greater emotional awareness by exploring the physical sensations accompanying your emotions or reflecting on the outcomes of your emotional responses. This enhanced awareness can lead to deeper insights and more meaningful changes in therapy.

As we continue to explore the lush landscape of EI and mental well-being, remember that each step you take to improve your EI is like planting a seed in your garden. With patience and practice, these seeds will grow, developing your ability to cope with mental health challenges and enriching your everyday life with more significant emotional clarity and resilience.

Managing Emotional Overwhelm with EI Strategies

Ever felt like you're juggling flaming torches while riding a unicycle, blindfolded? That overwhelming sensation isn't an overreaction—it's your brain's cry for a little emotional TLC. Emotional overwhelm can sneak up on us during high-stress situations or when life's demands get too intense. The good news? EI is the extra wheel ready to help. Let's identify these moments and how EI can stabilize overwhelming feelings.

First, spotting the signs of emotional overwhelm may be subtle, like snapping at your partner over something trivial, or it could be more apparent, like feeling paralyzed by your to-do list. Critical indicators of emotional overwhelm include irritability, anxiety, fatigue, and even physical symptoms like headaches or stomach aches. Recognizing these signs early is crucial because it's the first step in managing the overwhelm before it manages you. Think of it like catching a small leak before it becomes a flood—it's much easier to deal with when it's just a trickle.

Now, how can EI help manage these feelings of being overwhelmed? Every day overwhelmed might look hectic: emails pile up, your kids call for attention, and your mind becomes a whirlwind of tasks. Below are a few essential techniques that can be used to release pressure or act as a circuit breaker at those critical points.

1. A simple technique is the 5-4-3-2-1 method: Name five things you can see, four you can touch, three you can hear, two you can smell, and one you can taste. It's surprisingly effective at focusing your mind away from future worries or past regrets and bringing it back to the here and now.
2. Another EI strategy is emotional distancing. This doesn't mean disconnecting from your feelings. Instead, it's about stepping back to observe your emotions without judgment. By doing this, you can see your emotions as temporary states rather than defining aspects of who you are, which reduces their intensity and allows you to think more clearly about how to handle them. This would tie into the *self-regulation* component of EI.

Preventative practices are also a cornerstone of using EI to manage overwhelm. Regularly engaging in activities that nourish your emotional well-being can help maintain your equilibrium. This could be as simple as scheduling quiet time for yourself to read, meditate, or enjoy a hobby. It's about creating a buffer of calm around you that life's stresses can't easily penetrate. Just like you might take vitamins to fend off a cold, think of these activities as your daily dose of emotional wellness.

Lastly, always appreciate the power of a robust support system. This might be family, friends, or a professional therapist; having people you can turn to when you feel overwhelmed can make a difference. They provide perspective, advice, and sometimes just a listening ear when you need to vent. Building and maintaining these relationships is vital, not just for times of crisis but as an ongoing exchange of support and care.

Managing Stress and Anxiety with EI Techniques

Stress and anxiety are like those uninvited dinner guests who somehow always manage to eat up all your peace of mind. But what if you could develop a knack for spotting these gatecrashers from a mile away and had the perfect plan to handle them gracefully? That's where EI steps in as a skilled mediator who helps you maintain your cool in any situation.

Identifying stressors through EI starts with keen *self-awareness*. It would help if you tuned into those subtle hints your body and mind give you when stress is on the horizon. Signals might include tightness in your shoulders when deadlines loom or how you snap at your partner when you feel overwhelmed with family responsibilities. Recognizing these signals is the first step in managing stress effectively because it allows you to address the stressors before they escalate into full-blown anxiety.

Now, let's arm you with some emotional coping strategies. One powerful tool is emotional reframing. This involves changing your perspective on a stressful situation to view it in a more positive or neutral light. For instance, instead of panicking about a packed schedule, reframe it as a challenge you're well-equipped to handle. This shift in viewpoint can reduce the immediacy of the stress and help you approach the situation more calmly.

Another strategy is controlled emotional expression. Sometimes, the best way to handle stress is to let out those emotions in a controlled environment. This could mean venting to a friend, writing in a journal, or even shouting into a pillow. By expressing these emotions, you're not letting them bottle up inside, which can often exacerbate stress and lead to anxiety.

The role of EI in building resilience to stress cannot be overstated. Resilience is like your psychological immune system, giving you the strength to bounce back from setbacks and stress. EI boosts this resilience by enhancing your ability to manage emotions and maintain equilibrium in challenging situations. For example, using EI to stay connected with your feelings allows you to navigate stressful times without losing your emotional balance. This connection will enable you to recover from stress more quickly and emerge even more vital.

Lastly, let's discuss preventative measures for managing stress through proactive EI. One practical approach is proactive relaxation. This means regularly engaging in activities that calm your mind and lower your stress levels, like yoga, meditation, or deep breathing exercises. By making these practices a regular part of your routine, you prepare your mind and body to deal with stress more effectively when it does come. Another preventative measure is setting emotional boundaries. This involves knowing how much you can handle emotionally and learning to say no or step back when things become overwhelming. It's about protecting your emotional space, which can significantly reduce stress and prevent burnout.

By integrating these EI techniques into your life, you transform your approach to managing stress and anxiety. Instead of being at the mercy of these emotional disruptors, you become adept at recognizing, managing, and preventing stress, leading to a calmer, more balanced life.

The Role of EI in Overcoming Depression

Depression, like a shadow, can silently follow you, often unnoticed until the dim overcast it casts affects every corner of your life. EI can be your light, a powerful beacon that illuminates and helps you navigate the darkness. By understanding and managing your emotions, EI becomes a critical ally in the battle against depression, giving you the tools to recognize, confront, and diminish the pervasive impact it can have on your life.

The first step in using EI as a tool against depression is to become adept at identifying what triggers your depressive episodes. This process involves a high degree of *self-awareness*, one of the cardinal components of EI. For instance, you might notice that your mood tends to plummet during winter or that certain social situations leave you feeling particularly drained and low. By tracking these patterns, you can begin to predict potential downturns in your mood and take proactive measures to mitigate them. It's like being a weather forecaster for your emotions; knowing a storm is coming, you can prepare rather than be caught off-guard.

One thing is understanding your triggers, but managing them effectively is where EI shines. Let's say you identify that conflict at work is a trigger for your depression. With strong EI, you can approach these situations by setting clear boundaries, seeking to understand the emotional underpinnings of the conflict, or finding constructive ways to express your feelings and needs. This proactive approach can help you manage the situation to mitigate or reduce the likelihood of a depressive response. (Brackett, 2006)

When it comes to coping mechanisms, EI encourages strategies that are rooted in emotional understanding and regulation. One effective technique is emotional expression, which involves finding healthy outlets for your emotions. This could be through creative pursuits like painting or writing, which allows you to express your feelings and helps distract and calm your mind. Additionally, seeking social support is crucial. Depression can isolate you, making it feel as though you're trapped in a room with no doors or windows. EI teaches you to recognize when you need to open up to others, whether friends, family, or a support group, allowing their perspectives and support to air out the room and let the light back in.

Moreover, while EI offers robust tools for dealing with depression, it's also important to recognize when professional help is needed. Therapy can be invaluable, and EI can significantly enhance its effectiveness. For instance, if you're already skilled in identifying and expressing your emotions, you can enter therapy with a clear sense of what topics to address, making the therapeutic process more direct and potent. Furthermore, therapists often use techniques that help you develop greater EI, such as cognitive-behavioral strategies that teach you to challenge and change unhelpful cognitive distortions and behaviors. In this symbiotic relationship, EI and therapy complement and strengthen each other, providing a comprehensive approach to managing depression.

Navigating depression with EI is about building a deep, compassionate understanding of your emotional landscape and using that knowledge to take gentle but firm steps toward recovery. Each small step, recognizing a trigger, expressing your feelings, or seeking help, is a victory in the ongoing journey towards better mental health. Through EI, you equip yourself not just to fight against depression but to thrive despite it, cultivating a resilience that is both healing and empowering.

Self-care and Emotional Intelligence: Nurturing Your Emotional Self

In the hustle and bustle of everyday life, where deadlines, family responsibilities, and personal ambitions collide, it's easy to forget the one vehicle driving all your successes and experiences—yourself. Self-care is the premium oil your car desperately needs after hitting those high miles. Self-care might be indulging in a spa day or curling up with a good book, but it's also about regular maintenance of your emotional well-being, ensuring you're tuned up and ready to enjoy the journey. EI is pivotal in guiding you in what your mind and body need most.

Self-care and EI are intertwined more closely than spaghetti and meatballs. At its core, self-care is about being aware of and tending to your emotional and physical needs. This *self-awareness* is a fundamental aspect of EI. When emotionally intelligent, you're better equipped to pinpoint precisely what self-care you need. It could be a quiet evening alone when you're feeling overwhelmed or an energetic hike with friends when you're feeling down. EI helps you recognize these needs before they become dire, like catching a glimpse of your fuel gauge before you hit empty.

Self-compassion is another crucial practice, especially when you feel like you're not meeting your expectations. It's about treating yourself with the same kindness and understanding that you would offer a good friend. Setting boundaries is equally important. This means learning to say no or to step back when necessary, recognizing that your emotional health is a priority.

Balancing self-care with other life responsibilities can often feel like trying to solve a Rubik's cube—when you think you've got one side aligned, the other side goes awry. Here's where EI comes into play, helping you prioritize and manage your time effectively. It involves making conscious decisions about spending time aligning your activities with your emotional and physical needs. For example, if spending quality time with your family in the evening recharges you, EI would help you recognize the importance of wrapping up work emails by a specific time to safeguard this ritual. It's about making intentional choices that support your overall well-being, ensuring that self-care doesn't get lost in the daily shuffle.

Creating a personal self-care plan that incorporates these principles of emotional intelligence can transform this from a sporadic luxury into a consistent practice.

Start by assessing your current self-care habits:

- What are you doing well?
- Where could you improve?

Next, set clear, achievable goals. For example, you may want to incorporate 20 minutes of meditation into your morning routine or ensure you have two tech-free hours each evening. Whatever your goals, write them down and consider what steps you need to take to achieve them.

Remember, the aim is not to overhaul your life overnight but to integrate self-care in ways that feel doable and enjoyable. Regular check-ins on your progress can help adjust your plan, ensuring it remains aligned with your emotional needs.

THREE

Emotional Intelligence in Motion

If emotional intelligence were a dance, consider this chapter your invitation to the floor. It's about moving naturally to the rhythm of daily life. From negotiating peace between your squabbling kids to navigating the choppy waters of workplace politics, EI offers the grace and agility needed to handle each step confidently and with poise. Let's lace up our dancing shoes and discover how EI can transform ordinary interactions into genuine connections and informed decision-making opportunities.

Everyday Emotional Intelligence: Practical Applications

Daily Interactions

You're at a family dinner where the topic of politics, a notorious dinner table grenade, comes up. Tensions rise, voices get louder, and suddenly, you're not just passing the potatoes—you're passing judgments. Here's where your EI steps in. Practicing *empathy* through active listening allows you to truly hear the shared perspectives, enabling you to respond more thoughtfully. Perhaps it's saying, "I see where you're coming from," instead of, "That's the most ridiculous thing I've ever heard." This approach doesn't just keep the peace; it deepens understanding and respect among everyone at the table.

Now, let's translate this to a work scenario. You're in a meeting, and a colleague vehemently disagrees with your proposal. Instead of getting defensive, tap into your EI. Recognize your initial emotional reaction—maybe irritation or defensiveness—and consciously choose to set it aside. Respond empathetically, acknowledge your colleague's concerns, and ask clarifying questions. This method diffuses potential conflict and opens a pathway to collaborative problem-solving. By consistently applying these simple EI strategies in your daily interactions, you're not just avoiding conflicts but building more robust, resilient relationships.

Social Media as a Mirror

Social media is an interactive mirror, reflecting not just selfies and status updates but more profound glimpses into our personal and emotional worlds. Each like, comment, or share is a brushstroke in the portrait of our digital selves, often highlighting our emotional responses and tendencies. For instance, notice how a simple scroll through your feed can trigger emotions—from joy at a friend's good news to envy over another's vacation snaps. These reactions provide insights into our emotional triggers and patterns, serving as a real-time feedback loop on our emotional state.

This reflective quality of social media offers a unique opportunity to observe and refine our emotional habits, which requires *self-awareness* and *self-regulation*. By paying attention to what evokes strong emotions, we can start to manage how we interact with content that affects us negatively. For example, if political posts tend to make you angry or stressed, recognizing this pattern is the first step in deciding how to better engage with such content. Consider engaging in healthier discussions or choosing to step back when needed. In this way, social media can serve as a tool for enhancing *self-awareness* and emotional regulation, critical components of EI.

Decision Making

Decision-making might not just involve weighing pros and cons; it's also an emotional minefield. Emotions play a massive role in deciding on a new job offer or planning a family holiday. Here's where EI becomes your internal compass. For instance, consider you're offered a prestigious job requiring relocation. Instead of immediately jumping to a decision driven by the excitement of the offer, use your EI to evaluate how this change would affect your emotional well-being and your family. Reflect on questions like: How does the thought of moving make me feel? Anxious? Excited? Both? What are my family's thoughts and feelings about this move? This reflection allows you to make a decision that balances both logical considerations and emotional well-being, ensuring that your choice is one you can wholeheartedly embrace.

Social Responsibility

Now, let's put on our global citizen hats. EI pushes us beyond personal benefit to consider the broader impact of our actions. For example, think about the environmental implications of your daily choices. Using EI, you might recognize feelings of discomfort or guilt when you opt for convenience over sustainability. This awareness can motivate you to make more environmentally friendly choices, such as reducing waste or supporting green businesses.

Moreover, in a professional setting, imagine you're leading a project that could significantly affect your community. EI equips you to consider how decisions might impact the social and environmental well-being of the community. This might involve engaging with community leaders or organizing forums to ensure that voices from all community sections are heard and considered.

Through these practices, EI enables you to navigate your day with mindfulness, informed decision-making, and a conscientious approach to social responsibility in simple interactions, significant life decisions, or taking action on global issues. EI offers the tools to move through life with understanding, *empathy*, and responsibility. By integrating EI into your everyday life, you not only enrich your own experiences but also contribute positively to the lives of others, fostering a more understanding and connected world.

Harnessing EI for Life Transitions

Life is a bit like being an acrobat in a circus—constantly jumping through hoops, flipping through changes, and occasionally flying through the air, hoping to land gracefully. Transitions such as switching careers, moving to a new city, or adjusting to a new family dynamic are all hoops that life throws at us. EI is your safety net, ensuring you navigate these changes with agility and land on your feet.

Navigating transitions effectively with EI begins with *self-awareness*. This involves stepping back and evaluating your feelings about the upcoming change. Are you anxious about a career switch? Are you excited about moving to a new city? Or you're feeling a mix of both. Recognizing and acknowledging these emotions is crucial because it helps you manage them effectively rather than letting them manage you. For instance, if you're feeling anxious about a job change, EI can guide you to seek out resources like career counseling or networking opportunities, which can ease your transition and boost your confidence.

Adapting to change is a skill that EI can significantly enhance. It involves maintaining flexibility in your thoughts and behaviors—letting go of old patterns and embracing new ways of living or working. One effective EI strategy here is to practice cognitive reframing—changing your perspective on the change. Instead of viewing a move to a new city as losing touch with friends, for instance, see it as an opportunity to meet new people and experience new cultures. This shift in perspective can transform a potentially stressful transition into an exciting adventure, making the process smoother and more enjoyable. (Matsumoto, 2018)

Growth through change is the most significant gift of life's transitions. Each change, chosen or unexpected, tests different aspects of our EI and enhances our ability to handle future challenges. Reflecting on how you've managed past transitions can reveal how much you've grown. Maybe you dealt with a recent relocation more gracefully than five years ago, or perhaps you found that shifting family dynamics didn't rattle you as much as they once would have. These reflections boost your confidence and deepen your understanding of your emotional patterns, which is invaluable for personal growth.

By embracing these strategies, you harness the full power of your EI to not just survive but thrive through life's inevitable changes. Each change is an opportunity to strengthen your emotional skills, deepen your self-understanding, and enhance your ability to navigate future challenges. So next time life sends a hoop, remember: with EI as your safety net, you're more than ready to jump.

Emotional Intelligence in Times of Crisis

When the sea of life gets stormy, the captains who navigate the storm with poise often wield their EI like a seasoned mariner who uses his compass. In the throes of a crisis, a sudden corporate scandal, or a personal tragedy, leaders are suddenly thrust under a spotlight where every decision and reaction is magnified. Here, the core elements of EI, such as *empathy, self-regulation,* and *self-awareness,* become more than just interpersonal tools—they become the linchpins of leadership.

Consider a leader facing a significant data breach in their company. Panic and fear are natural first reactions that ripple through the ranks, but an EI leader counters this with a calm demeanor and clear action plan.

Empathy plays a crucial role here; the leader fosters a supportive environment that can weather the storm by acknowledging the team's concerns and validating their feelings. By effectively communicating with their team about what is known, what is being done, and what steps team members need to take, the leader mitigates chaos and instills a sense of stability. Supporting others during crises is where EI proves its mettle. Reading emotional undercurrents gives leaders the insight to offer practical and emotional support, a crucial aspect of sharpened *social skills*. Active listening is vital here. It involves genuinely hearing what team members say and what they might hold back. Are they scared? Confused? Demoralized? Recognizing and addressing these emotions can help alleviate stress and build a resilient team. Moreover, leaders can foster a culture of mutual support, encouraging team members to look out for each other and to speak up if they feel overwhelmed, ensuring that the burden of the crisis doesn't fall on one person. This approach helps manage the immediate situation and strengthens trust and loyalty in the team, which are invaluable in the aftermath.

Shifting our lens to *self-regulation*, this trait acts as the keel that keeps the ship upright even as waves crash against it. Building emotional resilience doesn't happen in the eye of the storm but is cultivated during calmer waters. This preparation involves regular self-reflection, stress management practices such as mindfulness or meditation, and a clear sense of purpose. When a crisis does hit, this groundwork allows you to remain anchored in your values and vision, enabling you to make decisions from a place of stability rather than reactivity. For instance, a manager who practices mindfulness can maintain perspective in high-pressure situations, allowing them to think more clearly and respond more effectively.

Lastly, the actual test of EI in the furnace of crisis is the ability to learn from adversity through *self-awareness*. Crises, while undeniably challenging, also serve as potent catalysts for growth. They can highlight areas of weakness in systems, processes, or leadership styles that go unnoticed during smoother times. An EI leader uses these insights to initiate changes. This is useful to avert future crises and evolve into a more decisive leader and a more cohesive team. Reflecting on how a situation was handled, what was learned, and how it can inform future strategies is an exercise in adaptive growth, turning tough lessons into stepping stones for future success.

Navigating through crises requires a blend of courage, clarity, and compassion—qualities that are deeply rooted in EI. By leveraging EI to lead with *empathy*, communicate effectively, support others, and learn from the process, leaders can guide their teams through turbulent times and emerge more robust and cohesive on the other side. As you continue to develop your EI, remember that it's not just about managing emotions; it's about harnessing them to lead, inspire, and thrive, even in the face of adversity.

Continuous Growth: The Never-Ending Dance of Emotional Intelligence

The beauty of EI is that it flourishes with continuous learning and adaptation. Think of yourself as a student in the ever-expanding classroom of life, where each interaction and experience offers a fresh lesson in EI. This lifelong learning process involves an openness to new ideas and strategies that can deepen your understanding of yourself and others. For instance, you might discover a book on emotional resilience that shifts your perspective or attend a workshop introducing you to new communication techniques. Each learning moment adds a layer of sophistication to your emotional repertoire, helping you navigate the complexities of relationships and personal challenges with greater ease and insight.

As life evolves, so do our roles and responsibilities, as well as our emotional needs and challenges. This dynamic landscape calls for the setting of new EI goals. Early in your career, your focus was on developing assertiveness and confidence. As you find yourself in a leadership role or juggling family dynamics, your EI goals might shift toward *empathy* and conflict resolution. Setting these new goals isn't just about acknowledging growth but actively steering it. It involves assessing where you are in your emotional development and determining where you want to be. Setting specific, measurable, achievable, relevant, and time-bound (SMART) goals can guide this process, providing clear milestones and the *motivation* to reach them. This is where the critical component of EI, *motivation*, comes into play. An example of setting a SMART goal for sharpening your EI could go like this: Enhance my emotional intelligence by improving my ability to recognize and regulate emotions in challenging situations through attending a workshop, reading two books on emotional intelligence, and practicing mindfulness techniques within three months.

However, as with any form of growth, there are moments when progress seems to stall. Plateaus in EI development are expected. Overcoming these plateaus requires a mix of self-reflection and proactive change. It might mean seeking new challenges that push you out of your comfort zone or revisiting foundational EI skills with a new perspective. The key is recognizing that these plateaus are opportunities to pause, reassess, and reinvigorate your journey. Rediscovering *motivation* can be as simple as setting a new goal that reignites your passion or connecting with a mentor who inspires you to see your emotional capabilities in a new light.

Seeking and integrating feedback is another critical aspect of continuous growth in EI. Feedback is the mirror that reflects your emotional strengths and weaknesses to you, and it's essential for fine-tuning your understanding and application of EI. Encourage colleagues, friends, and family to provide honest feedback on handling emotional situations.

- Do you listen effectively?
- Do you manage your stress in constructive ways?

This feedback can provide invaluable insights that highlight areas for improvement and reinforce practices that are working well. Integrating this feedback effectively involves humility and the willingness to change—a dance move that requires flexibility and resilience.'

As you continue cultivating your EI, remember that each day presents new rhythms to learn and new dances to explore. Whether you're stepping into a complex emotional waltz or a quick-paced samba of daily challenges, your growth in EI is a dynamic, ongoing process that enriches your entire life experience. Keep dancing to the beat of emotional growth, and let the music of life enhance your steps.

Integrating EI into Personal Values

Now, let's weave EI into the fabric of your values. Values are like the stars we navigate by; they shape our actions, reactions, and interactions. Integrating EI into these values enhances your ability to live by them more consistently and authentically. It starts with *self-awareness*—understanding what you truly value- honesty, *empathy*, or independence. EI invites you to reflect on how well your daily life reflects these values. Are you as empathetic as you aspire to be in your interactions? Does your pursuit of independence cause you to shun collaboration?

By using EI to align your values with your behavior, you create a life that feels more harmonious and purposeful. For example, if you value compassion, EI equips you to recognize when you might be reacting judgmentally towards someone's mistakes and adjust your response to one of understanding and support. It also allows you to communicate your values more effectively, fostering deeper connections with those who share or respect these principles. This alignment enriches your sense of self and enhances your interactions with others, creating a ripple effect of positivity in your personal and professional circles.

Holistic Well-being

Finally, let's consider the holistic well-being that EI nurtures. EI promotes a balance of mental, physical, and emotional health. It starts with *self-awareness*, helping you recognize the signs of mental fatigue or stress. This awareness prompts actions that prevent burnout, such as taking breaks, seeking support, or engaging in relaxing activities. On a physical level, being in tune with your emotions can motivate you to maintain your physical health through regular exercise, proper nutrition, or enough sleep, as physical well-being significantly affects emotional states.

By embracing EI in these various facets of life, you unlock a version of yourself that is more aware, balanced, fulfilled, and genuinely content. Whether reaching for the stars of self-actualization, aligning your steps with your core values, advancing steadily towards your personal goals, or nurturing your holistic well-being, EI is your steadfast companion, illuminating the path to a more prosperous, more rewarding life.

Section 2:

EMOTIONAL INTELLIGENCE & RELATIONSHIPS

FOUR

Emotional Intelligence in Personal Relationships

Let's face it: managing relationships is often less about grand gestures and more about the nitty-gritty of daily interactions. Emotional intelligence can help you decode a partner's silent treatment or understand a teenager's eye roll. This chapter will dive into listening with *empathy* in maintaining and developing relationships—an essential skill that can turn misunderstandings into opportunities for a deeper connection. So, buckle up! We are about to turn you into an EI ninja in the dojo of personal relationships.

Listening with Empathy: The Key to Deeper Connections

Let us dig deeper into active listening. Active listening involves making a conscious effort to hear the words another person is saying and the underlying and potentially complex message being communicated. Let go of the urge to respond to practice active listening immediately. Instead, focus on understanding their point of view. Nodding, maintaining eye contact, and even mirroring their expressions are all cues that show you are tuned in. This level of engagement helps de-escalate potential conflicts and opens up a dialogue conducive to mutual understanding and respect.

You are discussing with your spouse about where to spend the holidays. You are all geared up to push for a sunny beach getaway while they are dead set on a cozy mountain retreat. Before you know it, the conversation has turned into a tug-of-war with no winners in sight.

Now, rewind and inject a dose of active listening into the scenario. Active listening is about engaging fully with your partner's feelings and perspectives. It is like putting on a pair of high-definition headphones; suddenly, you are picking up on nuances you have missed—their longing for a quiet escape or perhaps a cherished family tradition.

Barriers to Effective Listening

Have you ever found yourself planning your following argument while the other person is still talking? Or getting distracted by a buzzing phone? These are classic signs of passive listening and are a barrier to effective communication. Other barriers include emotional biases and preconceived notions, which can cloud our ability to hear what is being said. For example, if you believe your teenage son is consistently irresponsible, you might dismiss his explanations for coming home late, which could be legitimate. Recognizing these barriers is the first step toward dismantling them.

To overcome these hurdles, consciously clear your mind and approach conversations with a clean slate. This means setting aside your judgments and giving the speaker your undivided attention. It can be challenging, especially if the topic stirs intense emotions, but the rewards in understanding and connection are well worth the effort. Let us apply the active listening technique to your teenage son arriving home late. Instead of giving him a talking-to or punishing him, sit and listen to what he has to say about why he came home late, as he may have a legitimate reason for it.

Practical Listening Strategies

Enhancing your listening skills can be as simple as implementing a few practical strategies. Paraphrasing is a powerful tool. It involves repeating what the person has said in your own words. This allows for clarification of any misunderstandings. For instance, saying, "So, what you are feeling is frustration because you think we spend every holiday with my family, right?" can open up a conversation about deeper issues that may not have been explicitly stated.

Asking open-ended questions is another excellent strategy for encouraging more profound revelation and sharing. Questions like "How did that make you feel?" or "What would your ideal solution be?" prompt more than yes or no answers and can lead to a more engaging and fruitful conversation.

Listening Beyond Words

Sometimes, what is not said is just as important as what is spoken. Non-verbal cues, such as body language, eye contact, and silence, can provide significant insights into the speaker's emotional state. For example, crossed arms might suggest defensiveness, while a lack of eye contact could indicate discomfort. Being attuned to these signals allows you to respond more appropriately and sensitively, enhancing the connection and trust between you and the speaker and further developing your *social skills* through reading non-verbal cues. An interesting 2006 study found that physicians who use nonverbal cues to communicate with their patients are rated far more favorably, were seen as more caring, and were less likely to have their appointments canceled. Inversely, the doctors "judged by raters to convey higher levels of dominance and lower levels of concern or anxiety in their voice tones were much more likely to have been sued than other physicians in the sample." (Sluyter, 2006, pp. 28-34) So, readers, take my word when I say that non-verbal communication is essential; it could be the thing standing between you and a lawsuit!

By mastering listening with *empathy*, you become a better communicator, more understanding, compassionate partner, parent, or friend. It's about tuning into the frequencies of emotions that words sometimes fail to convey, transforming everyday conversations into opportunities for deep, meaningful connections. So next time you find yourself in a conversation, try to listen with your ears and your heart, too.

The Role of Vulnerability in Building Strong Bonds

Let us chat about vulnerability, shall we? Yes, it is scary, but it is also where the magic of genuine connection begins. Vulnerability is about letting your guard down and sharing your true self — flaws, fears, dreams, and all. It is about being honest about your weaknesses and not just your strengths. The strength in vulnerability lies in its ability to break down walls. It transforms relationships from superficial exchanges to deep, meaningful connections. One way to think of vulnerability is that it lays the groundwork for people to have *empathy* with each other, one of the five critical elements of EI. Once your guard is let down a bit, you are better able to put yourself in the shoes of another. Think about a time when someone shared something deeply personal with you—that moment likely changed the dynamic of your relationship, bringing you closer and deepening your trust in each other.

Vulnerability is the key that unlocks authenticity. It is what makes interactions genuine. It is not about oversharing or emotional dumping; it is about honesty about where you are and how you feel. When you open up, it invites others to do the same, creating a space where genuine connection flourishes. This does not mean every conversation has to be a deep dive into your soul. It is about being authentic. This might look like admitting you are not okay or sharing your excitement about a new hobby. These moments of authenticity build the foundation of strong, resilient relationships.

Overcoming the Fear of Vulnerability

Now, if the thought of opening up makes you want to run for the hills, you are not alone. The fear of vulnerability is like that voice telling you it is safer to stay in the pool's shallow end. However, what are we terrified of? Judgment, rejection, or perhaps feeling exposed? These fears are deeply ingrained, but overcoming them starts with understanding that vulnerability is about courage. Recognizing that vulnerability does not always mean facing adverse outcomes is crucial. More often than not, it leads to greater *empathy* and closeness.

One way to overcome this fear is to take small steps. Start by sharing something small with someone you trust and observe how it feels. Another strategy is to reframe your thoughts about vulnerability. Instead of thinking of it as opening yourself up to hurt, consider it a step towards building more robust, honest relationships.

Vulnerability as a Bridge to Intimacy

Diving deeper into relationships, vulnerability is about sharing your joys, passions, and dreams. It's about letting someone else see what lights you up and what keeps you up at night. This sharing creates a bridge to intimacy, transforming acquaintances into confidants. Vulnerability allows for a unique kind of intimacy that's rooted in understanding and acceptance. It is the difference between someone knowing your favorite color and someone understanding why that color resonates with you so deeply.

This plays a pivotal role in romantic relationships. When partners can share their fears and insecurities as freely as their hopes and dreams, it creates a stronger, more empathetic bond. Each person becomes a safe harbor for the other, a place where they can be themselves without fear of judgment. This level of intimacy fosters a deep, enduring love that can weather life's storms.

Setting the Stage for Vulnerability

Creating a safe environment where vulnerability is welcomed and valued is essential. This means being intentional about listening and responding when someone shares a piece of themselves.

Start by being present. There are better times to multitask. Give the person your full attention, showing them that what they have to say matters deeply to you. Respond with *empathy* and without judgment. Avoid trying to fix the situation immediately, which can sometimes feel dismissive. Instead, acknowledge their feelings, validate their experiences, and thank them for sharing with you. It is about making the other person feel seen and heard.

Encouraging a culture of openness can also extend beyond personal relationships to include family dynamics and workplace environments. Regular check-ins where members share their feelings can cultivate a habit of openness in families. Leaders can set the tone in the workplace by sharing their challenges and learning experiences. This does not weaken their authority but humanizes them, making them more relatable and approachable.

In essence, fostering vulnerability is about nurturing the roots of solid relationships. It's about moving beyond surface-level interactions and diving into the heart of connecting deeply with another person. By embracing vulnerability, you enrich your relationships and empower others to share their true selves, creating a ripple effect of authenticity and understanding in your personal and professional circles. So, the next time you feel hesitant to share that part of you that feels too soft, silly, or serious, remember that in vulnerability lies the strength to forge resilient and advantageous bonds.

Navigating Conflicts with Emotional Intelligence

Conflict is inevitable in relationships, but just because it's inevitable doesn't mean it has to be destructive. Picture EI as your conflict navigator, helping you navigate disagreements without losing your cool or connection. With a focus on understanding and *empathy*, EI transforms potential relationship roadblocks into opportunities for growth and deepening trust.

The essence of using EI in conflict resolution lies in shifting the focus from winning the argument to understanding the perspectives involved. This shift begins with *self-awareness*—recognizing your emotional triggers during conflicts. Are you quick to get angry, or do you shut down? Understanding your patterns helps you manage your reactions and approach conflicts with a more precise, calmer mind.

Empathy also plays a starring role here. *Empathy* requires stepping into the other person's shoes, even if they might not fit perfectly. It supports you in trying to see the situation from their perspective and understand their feelings and needs. This doesn't mean you have to agree with them, but understanding where they are coming from can de-escalate tension and open up a dialogue based on mutual respect rather than resentment. For instance, if your partner is upset because you are spending too much time at work, acknowledging their feelings of neglect can be more productive than defending your work schedule.

Strategies for Healthy Conflict Management

Managing conflicts healthily is akin to navigating a minefield while blindfolded; it requires careful, considered steps. The first step is staying calm. Easier said than done, right? However, maintaining your composure is crucial. It prevents the emotional hijacking of your rational brain, keeping those fight-or-flight responses in check, critical aspects of *self-regulation*. Techniques like deep breathing or pausing the conversation to take a break can help maintain this calm. Remember, the goal is not to suppress your emotions but to manage them constructively.

Once calm, focus on the issue, not the person. This means discussing behaviors and situations rather than attacking each other's character. Use "I" statements instead of "you" accusations. For example, say, "I feel overlooked when decisions are made without my input," instead of "You never consider my opinions!" This approach keeps the conversation centered on resolving the issue rather than devolving into a blame game.

Communicating Needs and Boundaries

Clear communication is your best ally in resolving conflicts. It's about expressing your needs and boundaries clearly and respectfully. It would help if you had some downtime after work to decompress before engaging with family. Communicating this need helps set expectations and prevents misunderstandings that could lead to resentment. When discussing boundaries, be specific. Instead of saying, "I need space," try specifying what kind of space and when, like, "I need about 30 minutes to myself after work before I'm ready to help with dinner or homework."

The Role of Clarity in Communication

Clarity in communication acts like a lighthouse, guiding ships safely to shore. It ensures that your messages are preserved in a fog of assumptions and misinterpretations. This involves being explicit about what you think, feel, and need without assuming the other person knows or understands your perspective. It also means asking questions if you need clarification on their standpoint. Clarifying questions can prevent a lot of heartache. For instance, if your partner says they are fine, but their tone suggests otherwise, a clarifying question could be, "I heard you say you're fine, but I sense you might be upset. Want to talk about it?"

Seeking Win-Win Solutions

Finally, finding solutions that satisfy all parties involved is like hitting the jackpot of conflict resolution. It requires creativity, flexibility, and a commitment to the relationship over the ego. This might include compromise or finding a third path you have yet to consider. For instance, if you and your partner disagree on holiday destinations, a win-win solution might involve spending a few days at the beach and heading to the mountains. It's about meeting halfway, where both feel heard, valued, and respected.

Navigating conflicts with EI is not about avoiding disagreements but managing them to strengthen relationships rather than strain them. Focusing on understanding, *empathy*, and effective communication can turn conflicts into catalysts for growth and deeper connection. So next time a dispute arises, remember, it's not necessarily an obstacle; it is an opportunity to practice and hone your EI skills, making every resolution a step towards a more understanding and connected relationship.

Initiating and Deepening Friendships with EI

The Role of Self-disclosure

When planting the seeds of friendship, think of self-disclosure as the watering can that helps these relationships blossom. Sharing personal stories, thoughts, and feelings does more than pass information; it builds trust and intimacy, paving the way for deeper connections. Self-disclosure is a critical part of sharing your vulnerability with others, and it, as mentioned before, allows *empathy* to flourish in a relationship. Imagine you are at a new job, and you share a bit about your weekend hiking adventures during lunch. A colleague then shares their love for the outdoors. Suddenly, you're no longer just coworkers but potential trekking buddies. This simple exchange can lay the groundwork for a friendship based on mutual interests and shared experiences.

Self-disclosure, however, does not mean baring your soul at every turn. It's a technique where you gradually reveal more personal layers as trust grows, the skill we know as *self-regulation*. The key is reciprocity and timing. Sharing appropriately personal (but not too private) experiences when the moment feels right encourages others to open up in return, creating a loop of mutual sharing that deepens the connection. For instance, discussing a challenging personal project might resonate with someone who has faced similar challenges, fostering a sense of camaraderie and understanding. The link between self-disclosure in relationships and emotional intelligence lies in the ability to share personal stories and emotions judiciously, fostering trust, *empathy*, and deeper connections through reciprocal and timely sharing.

Empathy as a Foundation

Empathy, the ability to understand and share the feelings of another, is a crucial foundation for a strong friendship. It is what allows you to be present with your friends in their moments of joy and in their times of sorrow. Consider a friend who's going through a tough breakup. Your ability to empathize will guide you to respond in a way that acknowledges their pain without overshadowing it with your own experiences or hastily offered advice. This empathetic response makes your friend feel genuinely heard and supported, strengthening the bonds of friendship.

Empathy also extends to celebrating successes. When a friend achieves something significant, *empathy* genuinely drives you to share in their happiness. This shared joy multiplies the happiness while reinforcing the emotional connection, reminding both of you why your friendship is valuable. In moments like these, *empathy* acts as a binding agent that cements the foundation of lasting friendships.

Emotional Support Systems

Friendships are more than shared hobbies and interests; they're also vital emotional support systems. EI plays a crucial role in forming and maintaining these systems. Consider how varied our friends can be—some are great for a laugh, others for deep heart-to-heart conversations, and some for those moments when you need tough love. EI helps you navigate these different dynamics, enabling you to offer and receive support effectively.

Building these supportive networks involves recognizing and appreciating each friend's different roles in your life. Who can rely on you for honest advice, who will cheer you up without fail, and who can offer the sage wisdom you need? This discernment enhances the quality of the support given and received, making each friendship more fulfilling and resilient. In times of crisis or challenge, this network becomes your emotional scaffolding, providing strength and stability when needed.

Common Interests and EI

Shared interests often serve as the initial glue that binds people together, but EI can turn these casual connections into lasting friendships. Engaging in activities you both enjoy sets a natural backdrop for easy interactions, but your EI will allow you to deepen these interactions into meaningful relationships. For instance, joining a book club connects you with fellow literature lovers and opens the door to discussions about life, philosophy, and personal experiences related to the books you're reading.

Moreover, EI enables you to navigate the complexities of friendships that might only be based on one or two shared interests. It helps you manage and integrate different aspects of your personality that might not always align perfectly. This might mean agreeing to disagree on specific topics or focusing on what brings you together rather than what could drive you apart. Applying EI ensures that these friendships remain enjoyable and enriching despite differences, allowing you to grow individually and together within the safe space of your shared interests.

In essence, EI supports the development and maintenance of friendships. It can transform simple interactions into opportunities for deeper connection, *empathy*, and mutual support, weaving a tapestry of relationships that enriches your life and the lives of those around you.

Understanding and Being Understood: The Friendship Paradox

Have you ever found yourself in a friendship where, despite your best efforts, it feels like you're speaking different languages? This is the crux of the friendship paradox—the continuous dance between seeking connection and the nuances involved in achieving mutual understanding. At the heart of this paradox is our intrinsic desire for connection. We are, after all, social creatures wired for interaction. This longing drives us to seek out others who share our joys, understand our pains and can hop into the groove of our everyday lives. But as straightforward as that sounds, the rhythm of human relationships is often more complex, layered with individual emotions, experiences, and expectations that can subtly—or sometimes starkly—color our interactions.

Navigating this complexity requires active emotional engagement, a dynamic process in which you share your own emotions but also tune into and respond to your friends' feelings. A successful friendship requires attentiveness to subtle mood shifts, unspoken worries, and unexpressed joys. This level of engagement often leads to a deeper understanding of one another and more finely tuned *social skills*.

But here's where it gets tricky—the balance of self and others. How do you maintain your emotional boundaries while profoundly investing in someone else's emotional life? This balancing act is crucial because while *empathy* and engagement are the pillars of deep connections, losing yourself entirely in someone else's emotional narrative can lead to burnout and resentment. The key is to maintain a sense of *self-awareness*, recognize when the scales are tipping too much in one direction, and gently rebalance them. It's okay to step back when you need to recharge your emotional batteries. True friends understand and respect that need because they value your well-being just as much as you value theirs.

However, achieving this mutual understanding has its challenges. Barriers like miscommunication, assumptions, and past experiences can distort the lens through which we view our interactions. For instance, if your friends have let you down in the past, you might interpret a canceled plan as a sign of disinterest rather than a genuine scheduling conflict. Overcoming these barriers starts with cultivating a culture of open communication. Encourage honest exchanges where both parties feel safe to express their thoughts and feelings without fear of judgment. Employ clarity in your conversations to avoid misunderstandings—be direct yet kind, specific yet open-ended enough to invite dialogue.

A sound strategy here is the practice of regular check-ins. These can be informal catch-ups where you share updates about your lives and how you feel about the friendship. Are there things that need addressing? Are there boundaries that need to be redrawn? Though potentially awkward, these conversations are the bedrock of a healthy, understanding friendship. They clear the air and ensure minor miscommunications don't become significant grievances.

In essence, friendship is a beautiful, complex dance of give and take, speaking and listening, sharing and receiving. It's about finding that sweet spot where you feel understood and where you know, where the give-and-take feels balanced, and where the emotional connection thrives on shared interests and mutual respect and understanding. So, as you navigate through the twists and turns of your friendships, keep tuning into this intricate dance of emotions, and remember, every step taken in understanding and being understood is a step towards more profound, more meaningful connections.

EI Strategies for Sustaining Long-Term Relationships

Maintaining Emotional Connection

Relationships need to be tended to and lovingly nurtured. Maintaining emotional connections with your relationships over time requires dedication and adaptability.

One effective way to sustain connections is through the practice of check-ins. In romantic relationships, these check-ins can be as simple as asking, "How was your day?" and actively listening to the reply. Nurturing a long-term relationship doesn't necessarily require consistent grand gestures; it's the small, consistent acts of kindness and interest that keep the emotional connection alive.

Incorporating emotional intelligence strategies into everyday interactions, such as check-ins and active listening, can help partners stay attuned to each other's emotional needs and experiences. Couples can cultivate a sense of emotional closeness and intimacy essential for relationship satisfaction and longevity by demonstrating *empathy*, validation, and understanding during these moments of connection. Furthermore, by remaining curious about each other and engaging in new shared experiences, couples can deepen their emotional connection and create lasting memories.

Moreover, engaging in new activities together can also stimulate emotional connectivity. This could be taking a dance class, hiking a new trail, or cooking a complex recipe together; new experiences can create shared memories and bring a fresh spark to the relationship. Research suggests that individuals with higher emotional intelligence are better equipped to manage stress and adapt to new situations, which can be particularly beneficial when exploring unfamiliar activities with a partner. (Goleman, 1995) A study from the Journal of Marriage and Family found that married couples who do leisure activities together report far higher marital satisfaction than couples who partake in activities separately. (Crawford, 2002, 433-449) By approaching new experiences with a sense of openness, curiosity, and emotional awareness, couples can create a supportive and harmonious environment that fosters growth and connection. Couples can create lasting memories, strengthen their emotional connection, and nurture a sense of adventure and exploration in their relationship by combining new activities' excitement and the emotional insight gained through emotional intelligence. Embracing novelty and growth together can invigorate the relationship and foster a sense of vitality and passion to sustain long-term love and connection.

Navigating Romantic Relationship Challenges with EI

Every relationship faces its share of challenges, but navigating these obstacles with EI can turn potential conflicts into opportunities for growth. For instance, when financial stress tests your bond, instead of allowing anxiety to drive your interactions, use EI to discuss your fears and brainstorm solutions together openly. This approach fosters a team mentality where both partners work together against the problem rather than seeing each other as the problem.

Another common challenge in romantic relationships is navigating differences in communication styles or conflict resolution approaches. Couples with vital emotional intelligence can leverage their understanding of emotions to bridge communication gaps and find mutually beneficial solutions. For instance, instead of escalating disagreements into heated arguments, partners can use their emotional intelligence skills to actively listen, validate each other's perspectives, and seek common ground. Couples can constructively navigate conflicts and maintain a sense of emotional connection and intimacy by prioritizing empathy, respect, and effective communication.

In times of disagreement or emotional intensity, partners must recognize the signs of escalating conflict and proactively take steps to de-escalate the situation. By practicing emotional intelligence, individuals can identify their emotional triggers and communicate their need for a break calmly and respectfully. Pausing allows both partners to regulate their emotions, gain perspective, and approach the issue with renewed clarity and understanding. By prioritizing emotional self-care and mutual respect, couples can navigate challenges gracefully and strengthen their emotional connection.

The Role of Forgiveness

Forgiveness in a long-term relationship is like oil in an engine; without it, the engine seizes. Holding onto grudges or past hurt can harm your emotional health and also create a barrier to intimacy. Forgiveness in romantic relationships differs from other relationships as the emotional stakes are often higher, and the level of vulnerability and emotional investment is more profound, making forgiveness more complex and impactful. Forgiveness still requires letting go of anger and resentment, especially for past wrongs. It's important to understand that forgiveness is a process that often requires you to openly discuss the hurt and listen to your partner's perspective.

Approaching forgiveness with emotional intelligence means recognizing that forgiveness is more about freeing yourself from ongoing resentment than condoning hurtful behavior. It involves *empathy*—understanding your partner's human flaws and the context of their actions. This doesn't mean forgetting or dismissing your feelings but moving forward without emotional baggage. Discussing what each of you can learn from the experience and how you can avoid similar issues in the future can turn a painful experience into a stepping stone for growth. Establishing clear boundaries based on mutual respect and understanding can also play a crucial role in the forgiveness process, as emotional intelligence allows individuals to set healthy boundaries that protect their emotional well-being while fostering trust and intimacy in the relationship.

Growing Together

Growing together as a couple involves *motivation, self-awareness,* and *empathy*. EI is crucial in this process by enhancing individuals' abilities to understand and regulate emotions, empathize with their partner's perspectives, and communicate effectively. A shared life might mean aligning your individual growth with your growth as a couple. This might mean supporting each other's career aspirations, personal interests, or spiritual journeys. It means you celebrate each other's successes as if they were your own and provide comfort and encouragement during failures. This mutual support fosters a deep sense of partnership and shared purpose.

Setting shared goals begins with understanding your own and your partner's *motivations*. Whether planning to buy a home, travel to a new place, or start a family, working towards common goals can strengthen your bond. It's essential to discuss these goals and adjust them as needed regularly, ensuring they reflect both partners' aspirations and values.

Lastly, cultivating a culture of appreciation is vital. Regularly expressing gratitude for each other's efforts and qualities can reinforce a positive perspective on the relationship. It's easy to take each other for granted over time, but a simple "thank you" or "I appreciate you doing…" can make a significant difference in maintaining a healthy, loving relationship.

EI in long-term relationships is about understanding *empathy*, forgiveness, and growth. It's about navigating the complexities of life together with a heart full of love, a mind ready to understand, and arms open to support each other. As you continue to weave the tapestry of your relationship, let EI guide your stitches, creating a picture that is as robust as it is beautiful, filled with memories, laughter, and enduring love.

The Ripple Effect: Spreading EI in Your Circle

Imagine EI as a stone tossed into a still pond. The ripples created by this single action can spread far and wide, influencing both the immediate area and distant shores. This is the power of your EI within your social and professional circles. When you exhibit high EI, you're not just improving your interactions; you're setting a standard and subtly encouraging others to elevate their emotional responses.

Influencing Others

The influence you wield through demonstrative EI can be profound and far-reaching. Consider a typical day at work: By handling a stressful situation calmly and understanding, you resolve the issue more effectively and model a healthier way of dealing with stress to your colleagues. Similarly, in your personal life, when friends and family see you managing conflicts with compassion and understanding, they're more likely to adopt similar strategies in their own lives. It's about leading by example, and as your circle observes the positive outcomes of your EI-driven actions, they're encouraged to mirror these behaviors.

Creating Positive Environments

Your EI is essential to cultivating positive environments wherever you go. At home, this might mean creating a space where family members feel safe expressing their feelings without fear of judgment. This open emotional exchange fosters a supportive family unit that thrives on understanding and mutual respect.

In the workplace, your EI can help foster an environment that values open communication, emotional well-being, productivity, and efficiency. By addressing emotional issues openly and with *empathy*, you create a workplace where employees feel valued and understood, which can significantly boost morale and productivity. Similarly, your EI can encourage inclusivity and understanding across diverse groups in community settings, promoting a sense of community well-being and connectedness. Developing emotional intelligence enables individuals to create spaces where people feel safe and encouraged to open up, fostering environments of trust, understanding, and mutual support in both personal and professional settings.

Mentorship and EI

Mentorship is a powerful avenue for spreading EI. Mentoring others gives you a unique opportunity to directly influence and enhance their emotional skills. While it may transfer knowledge and skills, this relationship fosters emotional understanding and maturity. Consider a mentorship scenario where you guide a less experienced colleague through the nuances of managing client relationships. By focusing on EI aspects, such as understanding client needs and managing stressful negotiations with *empathy*, you equip your mentee with the tools to handle all future interactions effectively. This nurturing can create a lasting impact as mentees carry these lessons forward, applying them in various aspects of their lives and potentially mentoring others.

Collective Emotional Growth

Considering the broader implications, the collective growth in EI within a community or organization can lead to substantial positive changes. As individuals become more adept at managing their emotions and understanding those of others, the collective EI of the group elevates. This can lead to fewer conflicts, more collaborative problem-solving, and increased group cohesion and satisfaction. Moreover, in societal terms, higher collective EI can contribute to social harmony and understanding, as people are better equipped to handle interpersonal differences and conflicts. This growth improves individual well-being and enhances societal well-being, leading to a more empathetic, understanding, and connected community. In wrapping up this exploration of the ripple effects of your EI, remember that each interaction is an opportunity to influence and inspire. Your EI can initiate waves of positive change that extend far beyond the immediate context through direct mentorship, creating supportive environments, or simply leading by example. By fostering an understanding of and commitment to emotional growth, you contribute to personal or immediate relational improvements and broader societal progress —a testament to the profound impact of EI on our collective lives.

As we close this chapter and look towards the next, consider the vast landscapes of opportunity that your EI prepares you to navigate. From personal relationships to broader community interactions, the skills you cultivate through EI are invaluable tools that enhance the lives of those around you. Let's continue to explore, grow, and connect as we carry these lessons into every facet of our lives.

FIVE

Emotional Intelligence in Parenting

Parenting is not just about ensuring your kids eat their veggies and do their homework; it's like being an emotional coach, a cheerleader, and sometimes, a referee. It's a role filled with joy, challenges, and much learning—for you and your children. Emotional intelligence is your secret ingredient, transforming everyday parenting challenges into growth, understanding, and connection opportunities. In this chapter, we'll dive into how you can nurture this vital skill in your children, from their toddling years through the tumult of adolescence.

Teaching Kids Emotional Intelligence: A Parent's Guide

The journey of EI begins much earlier than you might think. From the moment children start observing and interacting with the world around them, they begin to form the foundational aspects of EI. These include recognizing and naming their emotions, understanding others' feelings, and learning appropriate responses. It's fascinating to watch a toddler progress from temper tantrums to being able to say, "I'm sad" or "I'm angry." This growth doesn't just happen; it's fostered by every interaction they have with their environment.

Role of Parents as Educators

As parents, you play a pivotal role in this developmental saga. As the primary influencers in your children's lives, your role in developing their EI is monumental. It's about intentionally teaching them emotions and how they can be managed and expressed healthily.

It starts with simple games like "Show me a happy face" or "What does a sad puppy look like?" These activities may seem basic but are critical stepping stones in helping children recognize and label emotions. (Sluyter, 1997) This makes learning emotions fun and allows toddlers to begin to recognize these emotions in themselves and others. As they grow into preschoolers, expand this by connecting emotions to reactions. For instance, "When you feel angry, your face looks like this [shows an angry face]," and you might want to stomp your feet. This might be followed by: "What can we do to feel better?" This sets the foundation for emotional regulation—a skill they'll thank you for in the future.

Understanding others' feelings involves being able to empathize and recognize the emotions of others. Children must learn to put themselves in someone else's shoes and understand what others might feel in different situations. For example, if a friend is crying because they lost a game, a child with a good understanding of others' feelings would be able to recognize that their friend is sad and might need comfort or support.

Learning appropriate responses to those feelings involves knowing how to react and behave in response to the emotions of others. This includes showing *empathy*, offering help or support, or simply being there to listen. For example, suppose a sibling feels frustrated because they can't figure out a puzzle. In that case, an appropriate response might be to offer encouragement or assistance rather than teasing or ignoring them.

As children grow, their ability to manage and express their emotions becomes more nuanced. This growth is significantly influenced by what they see and experience. For instance, when you express gratitude or apologize in front of your child, you're not just showing good manners—you're modeling how to manage emotions and social interactions. Modeling positive emotional interactions is crucial as you provide a live demonstration of EI in action. These are lessons that children absorb and mimic. (Denham, 2012)

Moreover, your guidance involves setting up an environment where emotions are openly discussed and respected. This could be as simple as having family meetings where everyone shares their feelings about a family decision. These practices help children understand that their feelings are valid and vital, which is essential for their emotional development.

Adolescence Challenges

Navigating adolescence can be like trying to steer a boat through stormy seas. The challenges of identity formation, the quest for independence, and the influence of peer pressure can all impact an adolescent's EI. During this critical phase, teens are figuring out who they are and where they fit in the world, and their emotional responses can be intense and sometimes overwhelming.

Here, EI becomes a crucial navigational tool. Teaching adolescents to manage their emotions involves helping them understand that while their feelings are valid, how they express them can significantly impact themselves and others. Open discussions about the consequences of impulsive reactions or the benefits of pausing to consider other perspectives before responding are vital in supporting EI development in adolescents. The importance of *empathy* is also a crucial lesson to revisit at this time. These lessons can help mitigate the emotional upheavals that often accompany adolescence.

Strategies for Supporting Youth

Supporting children and adolescents in developing EI requires a toolbox filled with strategies, patience, and many open conversations.

One effective strategy is role-playing. You can help your child navigate hypothetical situations by exploring different emotional responses and outcomes. For example, you might role-play a situation where a friend has said something hurtful, exploring other ways to express feelings and protect themselves without escalating the conflict.

Another strategy is encouraging reflective practices. This can be as simple as daily chatting about their emotions throughout the day and why. These conversations can help children and adolescents become more self-aware and capable of managing their feelings. Additionally, teaching relaxation techniques like deep breathing or mindfulness can help them calm down when emotions run high. (Cowell, 2018, 531–533)

In EI development, your parent role is challenging and profoundly impactful. By embedding EI into your daily interactions and teachings, you're nurturing future empathetic, resilient, and emotionally aware adults. As we continue to explore the nuances of EI in parenting, remember that each lesson taught, each emotion shared, and each challenge navigated together strengthens the emotional fabric that binds you and prepares your children to face the world with understanding and grace.

Emotionally Intelligent Strategies for Discipline

Integrating EI into your parenting disciplining techniques isn't just beneficial; it's essential in raising well-rounded individuals. Let's explore some age-appropriate EI skills you can foster at different stages of your child's development to promote emotional growth.

When it comes to discipline, which can often feel like navigating a minefield with any age group, the key is approaching it with EI. Instead of traditional punitive measures, think of discipline as a teaching moment. For younger children, instead of time-outs, try time-ins. Sit with them instead of sending them to sit alone when they misbehave. Discuss what happened and guide them through understanding their emotions and behavior. "What made you hit your brother? Were you feeling angry? What can we do next time you feel that way?" This helps them make sense of their emotions and teaches them how to handle them better in the future.

With older children and teens, discipline shifts toward conversations about consequences and responsibilities. It's more about guiding them to understand the impact of their actions and encouraging them to consider how they can mend the situation. "I understand you were upset, but using your phone at night has tired you in the mornings. What do you think we can do to solve this?" This nurtures their ability to assess their actions and develop responsibility.

In all of these strategies, from play with toddlers, discussions with teens, or empathetic discipline across all ages, the goal remains to embed EI into the core fabric of your parenting. By doing so, you're addressing immediate behavior and conflicts and equipping your children with emotional skills that will serve them well throughout their lives. As you continue to adapt these strategies to meet the needs of your growing child, remember that every moment of emotional learning is aimed toward an emotionally healthy, empathetic, and self-aware individual.

Building Resilience in Children Through Emotional Intelligence

Resilience might sound like one of those buzzwords tossed around a lot, but it's as essential as those multi-vitamins you sneak into their breakfast smoothie when it comes to kids. Resilience is the psychological muscle that helps children bounce back from setbacks and challenges: a scraped knee, a bad grade, or a tiff with a best friend. It's what enables them to emerge from these challenges stronger and wiser. And just like any muscle, resilience needs to be developed and strengthened. This development is deeply intertwined with EI, which provides the tools and skills necessary to face life's ups and downs with confidence and grace.

The Connection Between EI and Resilience

So, how exactly does EI lay the groundwork for resilience? Well, it starts with the ability to understand (*self-awareness*)

and manage one's emotions (*self-regulate*), two critical parts of the five components of EI, as we outlined in the first chapter. Imagine your child is frustrated because they can't solve a math problem. EI helps them recognize their frustration, understand why they feel this way, and manage those feelings without giving up. This is the core of resilience: facing a problem, handling the emotional response, and pushing forward rather than folding.

Moreover, EI also enhances a child's *empathy*, which is crucial for developing resilience. When children understand and empathize with what others are feeling, they're better equipped to handle interpersonal challenges and more likely to lend and seek support when needed. This supportive give-and-take is a cornerstone of resilience, making tough times seem less daunting when faced together.

Strategies for Building Resilient Kids

Now, how do we turn these concepts into actionable strategies? One effective method is to encourage problem-solving skills. Instead of swooping in to fix every issue your child encounters, guide them through finding a solution themselves. Ask open-ended questions like, "What do you think would happen if you tried this?" or "Can you think of a different way to handle this?" This approach boosts their EI by making them aware of their emotional responses but also empowers them to take charge of the situation, an essential aspect of resilience.

Another strategy involves fostering a growth mindset, which is the belief that abilities and intelligence can be developed through dedication and hard work. Teach your children that setbacks reflect not their capabilities but opportunities for growth. Celebrate efforts as much as outcomes, and share stories of personal and family challenges that were overcome through persistence and emotional awareness. These narratives can be incredibly motivating for kids, showing them that resilience is more than possible and deeply ingrained in their family.

Supporting Children Through Challenges

Supporting children through challenges is where your EI as a parent comes into play. When your child faces a setback, how you respond can either bolster their resilience or undermine it. Start by validating their feelings. It's tempting to say things like, "Don't be sad," but it's more helpful to acknowledge their disappointment, anger, or frustration. This validation shows that it's okay to feel these emotions and that you're there to support them through it.

Next, guide them in expressing these emotions constructively. This might involve drawing out their feelings, writing about them, or finding physical outlets like sports or play. Teaching them healthy ways to deal with emotions helps them cope with immediate challenges and builds long-term resilience.

Finally, always lead by example. Children are incredibly perceptive and often learn how to handle life's challenges by watching how their parents do it. Let them see you manage setbacks and stress with optimism and EI. Your behavior provides a template for them to emulate, reinforcing the resilience-building lessons you're teaching them.

By fostering EI, you equip your child with the tools to navigate life's complexities with assurance and agility. As we move forward, let these lessons in resilience and EI guide you and your children toward a future where challenges and successes are met with grace, understanding, and an ever-growing sense of capability.

The Transformative Power of Emotional Intelligence

"When awareness is brought to an emotion, power is brought to your life."

Tara Meyer Robson

It's very common for us to blame our experiences on our circumstances without realizing that we could do something about them. Emotional intelligence is one of the greatest tools we have at our disposal for making sure our experience is a good one. It's the answer to resolving conflicts quickly (and avoiding them in the first place), making decisions that will serve us, and accessing opportunities that will lead us to success – and it's something it makes sense for us all to work on. When you have a better understanding of your emotions and how to handle them, you begin to realize that you have a lot more control than you thought you did – and that, I think, is the real game-changer.

I'm so passionate about the transformative power of EI that I'm determined to share this guidance with as many people as I can. It has such a profound impact on both personal and professional development that it really does have the power to change your whole experience, and that's something I want for everyone. Now that you have a better understanding yourself, I'd like to ask for your help in spreading this information further… and the best part about it is that you can make a huge difference without spending more than a few minutes of your time on it.

By leaving a review of this book on Amazon, you'll help other people realize the power of EI and embark on their own transformative journeys.

Reviews are a great way of sharing information and inspiring others to embrace personal growth with confidence, knowing that there's guidance out there to help them every step of the way.

Thank you so much for your support. You're making more of a difference than you realize.

Scan the QR code below to leave your review!

SIX

Emotional Intelligence & Culture

Navigating the vibrant networks of global cultures can sometimes feel like trying to order your favorite coffee in a foreign language—both exciting and slightly perplexing. Just as a latte isn't the same in Rome as in New York, emotional expressions and the rules governing them differ wildly from one culture to another. (Matsumoto, 2018, 1345-1371) This chapter guides you to understanding these diverse emotional dialects and learning to speak them fluently, enhancing your cross-cultural communication skills. So, buckle up! We're about to take a tour through the fascinating world of emotional expressions across cultures, and trust me; it's a journey worth taking.

Understanding Emotional Expressions Across Cultures

You're at an international conference, ready to present your groundbreaking project. While some attendees nod vigorously in agreement, others maintain a poker face. Here's where understanding the diverse emotional languages of different cultures comes into play. In some cultures, openly showing enthusiasm and agreement is standard; in others, maintaining an impassive expression is a sign of respect and attentiveness.

These differences aren't just quirks—they're deeply rooted in cultural norms dictating which emotions are socially accepted in public. For instance, in many Western cultures, displaying happiness and openly sharing achievements is commonplace and often seen as a sign of confidence. Contrast that with many Asian cultures where humility is cherished, and overt displays of pride might be frowned upon. Recognizing these nuances is crucial for avoiding faux pas and building genuine connections. It's about reading the room, not just with your eyes, but with your emotional intelligence.

Cultural Norms and Emotional Display Rules

Each culture has its own set of unwritten rules about emotional displays, known as display rules. These rules guide when, where, and how it's appropriate to express emotions. For example, in Japan, there is a cultural norm called "tatemae" (facade), which refers to the behavior and opinions one displays in public, often hiding one's true feelings to maintain harmony and avoid conflict. (Hoffman, 2017) Conversely, Mediterranean cultures usually encourage expressive communication and the sharing of emotions, viewing them as a sign of authenticity and warmth.

Understanding these rules is like knowing the dress code for a fancy dinner party—you want to fit in and show respect without losing your style. It's about finding that sweet spot where you can express yourself authentically while being culturally sensitive. This balancing act is about more than making a good impression; it's about fostering an environment of mutual respect and understanding.

Misinterpretations and Assumptions

One of the most common pitfalls in cross-cultural interactions is misinterpretation. What's considered a warm gesture in one culture might be seen as overbearing in another. For instance, maintaining eye contact is a sign of sincerity in many Western cultures. However, in some Asian cultures, too much eye contact can be perceived as argumentative or disrespectful. (Wong, 2002, 243-274)

These misinterpretations often stem from our own cultural biases—what I like to call the "emotional accent" we all have. We interpret others' emotions through the lens of our cultural understanding unless we consciously adjust our interpretive frameworks. This adjustment begins with awareness and is honed through experience and education. Awareness of these differences allows us to pause and consider alternative interpretations rather than jumping to conclusions based on our cultural assumptions.

Adapting Emotional Intelligence Skills

So, how do you adapt your EI skills to be effective across different cultural landscapes? The first step is education—learn about the cultural norms of the people you interact with. This doesn't mean you must become a cultural scholar; even basic knowledge of cultural norms can significantly enhance your interactions. For instance, knowing the essential greeting customs, whether a handshake, bow, or cheek kisses, can start your interaction on the right foot.

Next, practice active *empathy*. This means understanding the cultural context of their behavior and responding appropriately. This could involve moderating your emotional expressions to better align with the cultural norms of your counterparts. This will be further discussed with actionable techniques in the next section.

Lastly, embrace flexibility, which ties back to the EI component of *self-regulation*. The ability to adapt your emotional responses based on the cultural context is a powerful tool. It shows respect for other cultures and enhances your ability to communicate effectively. This flexibility isn't about suppressing your emotions but rather about expressing them in a culturally attuned and respectful way.

By mastering these skills, you enhance your personal and professional relationships and become a bridge-builder, connecting diverse cultures through the power of EI. This might be useful when negotiating a contract, working on an international team, or enjoying a multicultural festival. Your ability to navigate the emotional landscapes of different cultures can turn every interaction into an opportunity for learning, connection, and growth.

Cross-cultural Empathy: Building Bridges, Not Walls

Empathy, the ability to understand and share the feelings of another, doesn't just stop at the borders of your own culture; it extends its hand across seas, mountains, and deserts, reaching into the hearts of those whose lives may look vastly different from yours. This extension of *empathy* beyond our immediate surroundings is what we call cross-cultural *empathy*. The bridge connects disparate cultural islands, making our global village more cohesive and harmonious. But why is this so crucial? In a world as interconnected as ours, where businesses operate across continents and social networks span the globe, stepping into someone else's cultural shoes can mean the difference between a successful collaboration and a diplomatic faux pas.

However, building these bridges can be complicated. The challenge often lies in the subtleties of cultural nuances that can make the same gesture endearing in one culture and offensive in another.

Practical Steps for Enhancing Cross-cultural Empathy

Actively practicing *empathy* involves a deeper engagement with diverse cultures. A practical step for enhancing cross-cultural *empathy* is learning a new language. This is an excellent way to dive deep into the cultural psyche, as language often reflects the values and priorities of its speakers. It also involves participating in cultural exchange programs, which could be through work, school, or volunteer opportunities, which can provide firsthand experience of other cultures. These immersive experiences allow you to see the world through others' eyes, fostering a deeper, more genuine understanding and appreciation of their emotional landscapes.

Expanding your cultural consumption is another strategy to support active cross-cultural *empathy*. Dive into books, films, and music from other cultures. This form of emotional education offers insights into what people from different cultures fear, love, and aspire to. Next, engage with individuals from other cultures in your community. Attend cultural festivals, join international clubs, or volunteer for organizations that work with diverse groups. Each interaction is an opportunity to practice *empathy*, learn and unlearn, connect, and sometimes listen.

Another practical step is reflection. After interacting with someone from a different culture, take a moment to reflect on the experience. What did you learn about their emotional perspective? What surprised you? What challenged your assumptions? This reflective practice deepens your understanding and prepares you for more meaningful future interactions.

Case Study of Successful Cross-cultural Empathy

One inspiring example comes from the world of non-profit organizations. A group focused on educational outreach in Central Asia found that its initial programs were met with resistance from local communities. They reevaluated their approach, starting with extensive dialogues with community leaders and immersive stays by the program designers within the community. By genuinely understanding and integrating the community's cultural and emotional frameworks, the organization redesigned its programs to be more culturally congruent. The revamped programs were not only welcomed but became self-sustaining within the communities. (Brackett, 2014, 120-138)

This case study highlights the transformative power of cross-cultural *empathy* both in corporate and community settings. The ability to empathize across cultures builds lasting relationships and fosters mutual respect and understanding. As you continue to navigate the rich diversity of our world, remember that each step toward enhancing your cross-cultural *empathy* brings us all closer to a more connected and empathetic global community.

Multicultural Relationships: The EI Guide to Harmony

When we dive into the complexities of multicultural relationships, it's crucial to recognize that each culture brings its values, beliefs, and communication styles to the table. Imagine a scenario where you, someone raised in a straightforward communication culture, are partnered with someone whose background emphasizes more nuanced, indirect ways of expressing disagreement. Without a keen sense of EI, it's easy to see how quickly misunderstandings can spiral. Here, EI steps in as a mediator, helping you decode the unspoken, understand the why behind the what, and respond in a way that respects your perspectives.

Building cultural competence becomes an essential skill in your EI toolkit. EI enhances understanding how cultural norms influence thoughts, emotions, and behaviors. Developing this competence involves continuous learning and exposure. Engage with diverse cultures through literature, films, food, and, most importantly, conversations with individuals from different backgrounds. Each interaction is a piece of the puzzle, helping you build a clearer picture of how various cultural frameworks operate.

Communication Strategies for Multicultural Relationships

Effective communication in multicultural settings requires a blend of active listening, *empathy*, and adaptability. Start by listening—not just to the words being spoken but to the context in which they are said. Pay attention to non-verbal cues, often telling you more about a person's feelings than words. For instance, if someone from a high-context culture (where much is communicated through non-verbal cues) seems uncomfortable, they might not outright say it, but their body language—avoiding eye contact and closed body posture—will give you clues.

Empathy, too, plays a pivotal role. It allows you to see the world through your partner's or colleague's cultural lens. When discussions about sensitive topics like politics or religion arise, *empathy* enables you to navigate these conversations without turning them into conflicts. Remember, it's not about agreeing with everything but understanding where they come from.

Flexibility in your communication style is equally critical. Be willing to adapt your style to better align with others'. For instance, if you're working with someone from a culture that values formal communication, mirroring this formality can show respect and foster a smoother interaction.

Case Examples

Let's consider a couple, Anna from Sweden and Tomo from Japan. They exemplify the successful navigation of a multicultural relationship through EI. Anna's Swedish upbringing instilled a straightforward, egalitarian approach to communication, while Tomo was accustomed to a more hierarchical, indirect communication style. Early in their relationship, Anna's directness comes off as careless to Tomo, while Tomo's subtlety is confusing to Anna. However, by actively learning about each other's cultural backgrounds and employing EI—particularly in *empathy* and active listening—they learned to interpret each other's communications accurately and appreciate their underlying intentions. Their relationship thrived as they developed a new, shared communication style that blended both cultures. (Gottman, 2016)

This example illustrates the potential challenges in multicultural relationships and the profound growth and harmony that can be achieved through applying EI. As you continue to interact and build relationships across different cultures, remember that, like any good dance, it's about finding the rhythm and harmony in your movements. In a romantic partnership or a professional collaboration, the EI strategies discussed here can genuinely guide you in understanding and celebrating your cultural diversities.

As we wrap up this chapter, remember that the beauty of our world lies in its cultural diversity. Embracing this diversity through EI enriches our personal and professional lives and contributes to a more empathetic and understanding global community. Let this understanding guide you in every new cultural encounter, turning each interaction into an opportunity for growth, connection, and mutual respect. The next chapter will explore how EI interacts with technology, where cultural and emotional nuances meet the digital age.

SEVEN

Emotional Intelligence & Technology

Navigating the digital world can sometimes feel like trying to read a book in a language you're only halfway fluent in. You catch the gist, but the subtleties? They could be in hieroglyphics. In hyper-connected lives, where emojis replace expressions and texts replace talks, understanding and conveying emotional intelligence online becomes just as crucial as face-to-face. Indeed, technology can be utilized to support us in connecting better. Let's unpack the art of digital *empathy* in maintaining relationships, explore how to enhance your digital communication skills, and delve into digital spaces' role in providing emotional support.

The Challenge of Empathy Online

A friend you're texting has just lost their job. You want to express your concerns and support, but you fear that your "I'm so sorry!" text might come across as insincere or, worse, a generic response you just copied and pasted. Here lies the crux of digital *empathy*: the challenge of expressing and interpreting emotions accurately without the benefit of vocal tone, facial expressions, or body language. These cues, which we often take for granted, are the backbone of understanding each other's emotional states. Without them, even well-intentioned messages can misfire spectacularly.

In the digital realm, where communication is often reduced to text and images, misinterpretations are rife. The tone could be more accessible to convey and more straightforward to interpret. Is that period at the end of a sentence a sign of anger, or just proper punctuation? The ambiguity can be a minefield. Plus, the brevity favored in digital communication often strips away the nuance necessary for understanding complex emotional states. This can make deep, empathetic connections harder to forge and maintain. But fear not, we're not doomed to a world of misunderstood texts and emoji confusion. The development of digital *empathy* skills can bridge this gap.

Building Empathy Through Digital Platforms

So, how do we cultivate *empathy* and maintain relationships in a space where "LOL" can mean anything from genuine laughter to passive aggression? First, it's about mindful communication. Take an extra moment to consider how your words might be perceived. Does your message convey what you intend? Could it be read differently? This mindfulness turns sending a text, email, or social media comment from a reflex into a thoughtful process.

Second, use the available tools to add warmth and clarity. When used appropriately, emojis, GIFs, and memes can enrich the text and help convey tone and emotion. For example, a well-placed smiley face can soften a statement that might otherwise seem stern. Beyond emojis, consider using video messages or voice notes when text alone doesn't suffice. Hearing your voice or seeing your face can make all the difference in conveying genuine *empathy*.

Digital Communication Skills

Effective emotional communication in the digital world also involves transparency and openness. Since digital communication lacks the immediate feedback of face-to-face interactions, clarity becomes paramount. Be explicit about your feelings and ask openly about theirs. Phrases like "I'm excited about this!" or "I'm feeling unsure about your last message; can you clarify?" can guide the emotional tone of the conversation and invite openness from the other side.

Moreover, active listening—yes, even online—is vital. This can mean acknowledging messages with more than an "okay" or a thumbs-up. Provide thoughtful responses that show you are engaging with the content of the conversation. This engagement demonstrates that you are investing in the relationship, not just maintaining it.

A growing body of research is finding that digital emotional intelligence is not just "EI in a digital world" but rather its unique classification when it is integrated with the concept of "digital competence," a trait that many young people have and is now seen as not just a right but a requirement of citizens. Digital competence encompasses the skills people have to function in a digital world, knowledge, and attitudes. (Audrin, 2023)

The Role of Digital Spaces in Emotional Support

Online communities and forums present unique spaces where individuals can find support and understanding from others with similar experiences. This is vital in generating relationships and also serves as a self-reflective tool. Digital spaces often provide a sense of anonymity and safety that can encourage openness and vulnerability. For instance, someone struggling with mental health may find it easier to first express their feelings in a supportive online group before talking to someone face-to-face.

These communities can be precious in extending support networks beyond geographical limitations. Whether it's a forum dedicated to new parents, a support group for anxiety, or a network for professional women, these spaces offer opportunities for emotional support, advice, and solidarity. By participating in or moderating such communities with *empathy* and respect, you contribute to a supportive digital environment where EI thrives and acts as a learning environment, which might prompt reflective thinking.

By embracing these strategies, you contribute positively to the broader digital world. As we navigate this interconnected digital landscape, let's commit to being architects of understanding and *empathy*, building bridges that connect us meaningfully, no matter the physical distance.

Using Technology to Enhance Self-Awareness and Self-Regulation

In the digital age, where our lives often feel like an episode of "Black Mirror," technology isn't just about staying connected; it's also about becoming more reflective and in control. Imagine having a personal coach nestled in your pocket or wrist, gently nudging you towards better emotional health. That's what modern apps offer—a digital nudge towards greater *self-awareness* and *self-regulation*. Let's explore how these tools are innovative and EI, helping us to tune in better to our inner worlds.

Apps for Emotional Intelligence

Think of apps as the Swiss Army knives in your emotional toolkit. With the right app, your smartphone can be a powerful ally in enhancing EI. For instance, consider an app designed to help you track your mood swings. By regularly logging how you feel, you can begin to notice patterns and triggers in your emotional landscape. For example, apps like Moodpath and Daylio help you track your mood and provide insights into your emotional patterns and behaviors over time. By understanding your emotions more deeply, you can communicate more effectively with your loved ones and navigate conflicts with greater *empathy* and *self-awareness*.

Apps like Headspace and Calm offer mindfulness and meditation practices that enhance emotional intelligence and benefit relationships. By cultivating mindfulness through these apps, you can develop a greater sense of presence and emotional regulation, leading to more meaningful and connected interactions. Practicing mindfulness can also help you become a better listener, respond more thoughtfully in conversations, and be more attuned to the emotions of those around you.

Furthermore, relationship-building apps like Gottman Card Decks provide tools and exercises to strengthen communication skills, build trust, and deepen intimacy in romantic relationships. These apps offer practical strategies for resolving conflicts, expressing appreciation, and fostering emotional connection with your partner. By incorporating these apps into your daily routine, you can proactively work on improving your emotional intelligence and nurturing healthy, fulfilling relationships.

Utilizing these apps as part of your emotional toolkit can enhance your emotional intelligence and create a more supportive and empathetic environment in your relationships. These apps serve as valuable resources for self-reflection, growth, and communication, empowering you to cultivate stronger emotional connections and navigate the complexities of human relationships with greater understanding and *empathy*.

Online Journals and Diaries

Moving from a little screen to a bigger screen, online journals and diaries offer a digital canvas for our thoughts and feelings. In the hustle of everyday life, taking a moment to jot down your thoughts can be a soothing balm for a busy mind. These digital platforms offer more than privacy and convenience; they provide tools for tagging and tracking emotional entries, enabling you to observe trends over time. Apps like Day One and Penzu are examples of online journals and diaries that offer features for tagging and tracking emotional entries. These apps allow users to categorize their thoughts and feelings with specific tags, making identifying patterns and trends in their emotional experiences easier. Reflecting on your entries can enhance *self-awareness*, offering insights into your emotional responses and how they shape your daily experiences. This practice can be particularly transformative, turning abstract feelings into concrete words, often making them easier to understand and manage. This enhanced *self-*

awareness can also lead to more authentic and meaningful connections with others as individuals become more attuned to their emotions and how they influence their relationships.

Navigating Social Media with Emotional Intelligence

Using social media with EI involves more than just managing our reactions; it's also about contributing positively to the digital ecosystem. This means thinking twice before reposting sensational news or engaging in heated debates. It's asking ourselves, "Is this contributing to meaningful dialogue? Am I adding to the noise or the harmony?" By applying principles of EI, such as *empathy* and mindfulness, we can create more thoughtful, respectful interactions online. Being mindful of the tone and content of our social media posts can significantly impact how others and the quality of our relationships perceive us. Clear and empathetic communication online can prevent misunderstandings, build trust, and maintain genuine connections that mirror real-life relationships. By infusing our digital interactions with *empathy* and respect, we can cultivate a digital environment where meaningful relationships thrive and authenticity and understanding prevail.

For instance, considering the person's emotional state behind a post before commenting can lead to more supportive and empathetic interactions, strengthening relationships and promoting a culture of online understanding and support. Clear communication, infused with *empathy*, can go a long way in maintaining digital relationships that are as respectful and genuine as those in real life.

The Influence of Social Media on Emotional Well-being

The influence of social media on our emotional well-being extends to our relationships with others, shaping how we perceive ourselves and interact with those in our social circles. The curated perfection often portrayed on social media platforms can lead to feelings of inadequacy, comparison, and jealousy, affecting our self-esteem and engagement with others. By being selective about who we follow and setting boundaries on our social media use, we can create a healthier online environment that supports our emotional well-being and fosters more positive and authentic relationships with others.

A study from researchers at the University of Hagen found a significant difference in the relationship between EI and Facebook use based on age groups. Younger individuals showed a positive relationship between EI and Facebook use, while older individuals exhibited a negative relationship. The paper explained the disparities in EI by postulating that "members of a younger cohort use Facebook more and are accustomed to it, as they grew up with social media (Bolton et al., 2013). They possibly develop their EI through or along with social media use and through social networks, while the older cohort is alienated by the frequent superficial relationships on Facebook with increasing EI." (Hornung, 2018)

Balancing our screen time and being intentional about our social media use can directly impact the quality of our relationships online. By engaging with content that inspires and uplifts us, we can cultivate a digital space that promotes positivity and connection. Setting boundaries around social media usage helps prevent it from consuming our lives and allows us to prioritize real-life interactions and emotional well-being. Taking regular digital detoxes when needed can also be beneficial in resetting our relationship with social media and ensuring that it enhances rather than detracts from our emotional health and connections with others. This requires a degree of intentionality and *motivation*, as you are not seeking a reward in your digital detox. However, instead, you are choosing to discern and disconnect for your mental well-being.

Artificial Intelligence and Understanding Human Emotions

Artificial Intelligence (AI) has significantly advanced in recognizing and interacting with human emotions, transforming how we understand EI in the digital age. AI is a branch of computer science that focuses on creating machines capable of intelligent behavior. As you may have experienced, AI technologies are no longer confined to rigid computational tasks but have evolved to encompass more nuanced human-like interactions. This progression stems from a growing field known as affective computing, which aims to develop systems and devices that can recognize, interpret, process, and simulate human effects—the experience of feeling or emotion. The connection between AI and emotional intelligence lies in AI's ability to recognize and respond to human emotions, contributing to the development of emotionally intelligent systems that can understand and interact with users in more human-like ways.

The role of AI in emotional recognition is profound. As AI technologies become more adept at understanding human emotions, they are increasingly utilized in various contexts to enhance relationships. In personal interactions, AI-powered tools can analyze emotional cues in conversations, helping individuals communicate more effectively and empathetically in a way that develops their own set of *social skills*. In professional settings, AI-driven systems can improve team dynamics by facilitating better understanding and collaboration among colleagues, increasing productivity and job satisfaction.

The relationship between AI and EI is poised to become increasingly complex and influential. On the one hand, the potential benefits are vast. AI could revolutionize mental health care by providing new tools for diagnosis and treatment, aid in educational settings by adjusting teaching methods to students' emotional states, and improve workplace productivity and satisfaction by fostering better communication and understanding among team members. On the other hand, the challenges are equally significant. Ensuring that AI systems handle emotional data ethically and responsibly will be paramount.

As we continue integrating AI into more aspects of our personal and professional lives, it becomes crucial to foster a deeper understanding of how these technologies work, their potential, and the challenges they present. This understanding will be essential as we navigate the increasingly blurred lines between human and machine, emotion and algorithm.

The Neuroscience Behind Emotional Intelligence in Digital Interactions

The fusion of neuroscience and technology has opened fascinating avenues for understanding how our brains interact with digital environments, mainly through advancements like brain-computer interfaces (BCIs). (Hoffman, 2017, 3111-328) These interfaces facilitate a direct communication pathway between the brain and an external device, allowing thoughts to control computers, prosthetics, or other technologies without physical movement. This remarkable capability enhances the lives of those with mobility impairments and offers profound insights into the neural underpinnings of human-computer interaction. We can decipher how thoughts and emotions manifest neurologically when engaging with digital technologies by capturing brain signals.

BCIs are particularly intriguing when considering their role in EI within digital contexts. For example, these devices can measure the brain's response to various stimuli in a virtual environment, providing real-time data about emotional engagement and cognitive load. This capability could transform how we design digital content, making it more adaptive and responsive to the user's emotional state. Imagine a learning platform that, through BCI integration, recognizes when a user feels confused or stressed and automatically adjusts the information's complexity or the instruction pace. Such responsive systems could significantly enhance learning efficiency and personalization, making digital interactions more intuitive and empathetic aligned with users' emotional needs. Furthermore, when considering the intersection of BCIs and emotional intelligence, particularly in the realm of *self-awareness* and reflection, these devices have the potential to provide individuals with valuable insights into their own emotional responses and cognitive processes. By leveraging BCIs to monitor and analyze brain activity related to emotions and *self-awareness*, users can better understand their inner states and behaviors, ultimately fostering greater self-awareness and emotional regulation.

Further exploring the realm of emotional processing, it's fascinating to consider how our brains handle emotions differently when interacting within digital versus physical environments. Studies indicate that some brain regions, including those involved in *emotional regulation* and *empathy*, respond uniquely when we engage with digital media. For instance, virtual settings might not activate mirror neurons —responsible for *empathy* and understanding others' emotions—to the same extent as face-to-face interactions. This distinction suggests that while digital platforms can simulate social interactions, the emotional depth and quality can differ significantly from those experienced in real life. Understanding these differences is crucial as we increasingly rely on digital communication tools for significant and impactful human interactions, from remote work meetings to telehealth psychology sessions.

The Double-edged Sword of Connectivity

Social media offers the incredible ability to connect with people worldwide, breaking down geographical and cultural barriers. This connectivity fosters *empathy*, broadens perspectives, and builds a global community. On the flip side, the same connectivity can lead to information overload, privacy issues, and an increased sense of isolation—paradoxically, as we connect more online, we can sometimes feel more alone. When interacting with strangers anonymously, online anonymity can reduce our overall *empathy* for those we are communicating with, leading us to say things we would never say to someone in person.

Navigating this double-edged sword requires a conscious approach to social media. Embrace its benefits to enhance your understanding of diverse cultures and global issues while being aware of its potential to cause stress or feelings of disconnection. Engaging with social media should be different from face-to-face interactions but complement them, enriching your relationships and understanding of the world. In turn, you will develop a whole new set of *social skills* accompanying the face-to-face kind.

Teaching Digital Emotional Intelligence

In the digital age, teaching EI must extend to the virtual environments where children and teenagers spend a significant portion of their time. Educating the younger generation on using social media responsibly and empathetically is crucial. This education should focus on understanding online interactions' emotional impact and *empathy*'s importance in digital communications.

Parents and educators can lead by example, demonstrating healthy social media habits and discussing the emotional aspects of digital interactions. Encouraging young people to reflect on how their online behavior affects themselves, and others can cultivate a more mindful and empathetic approach to social media use. Moreover, teaching emotional intelligence to children and teens includes guiding them on interacting with their peers online in emotionally intelligent ways. This involves emphasizing the significance of *empathy*, active listening, and respectful communication in digital interactions. By fostering these skills, young individuals can build stronger and more positive relationships in the digital realm, promoting a culture of kindness and understanding in online communities. (Gottman, 2016)

As we close this chapter on the intersection of EI and technology, remember that each tool, platform, or app offers unique opportunities for emotional growth and connection. Whether reflecting on your emotional patterns through social media, managing stress with wearable tech, or enhancing *empathy* through virtual reality, technology can be a powerful ally in your EI journey. As we transition into the next chapter, let's carry forward the commitment to use technology to connect more and better.

Section 3:

EMOTIONAL INTELLIGENCE IN THE WORKPLACE

EIGHT

Emotional Intelligence & Career Development

Using EI to Blaze a Career Path for Yourself

Emotional intelligence plays a crucial role in choosing a career path and building a successful future. By understanding and managing one's own emotions and being attuned to the emotions of others, one can make informed decisions that align with one's values, interests, and strengths.

Emotional intelligence can help you assess your passions and goals more effectively when choosing a career path. For example, by being *self-aware* and understanding your *motivations*, you can identify the type of work that excites and fulfills you. This *self-awareness* can guide you toward a career that matches your skills and resonates with your values and long-term aspirations.

Furthermore, emotional intelligence enables you to navigate the complexities of the job market and workplace dynamics. For instance, by developing strong *social skills* and *empathy*, you can build relationships with mentors, network effectively, and collaborate with colleagues to foster growth and advancement in your chosen field.

Emotional intelligence can help you adapt to challenges, setbacks, and changes in the professional landscape when building a future for yourself. By managing stress, staying resilient, and maintaining a positive outlook, you can overcome obstacles and seize opportunities for career development and personal growth.

Acing the Interview

When it comes to acing a job interview, emotional intelligence can be your secret weapon to showcase professionalism, confidence, and *empathy*, ultimately helping you secure the job offer you deserve. By understanding the wants and needs of your potential employer, you can tailor your responses and demeanor to make a lasting impression and stand out from the competition.

During an interview, EI allows you to connect more deeply with the interviewer, showing genuine interest in the company's values, culture, and goals. By actively listening, maintaining eye contact, and mirroring the interviewer's body language, you can build rapport and demonstrate your ability to communicate effectively and empathetically.

Moreover, EI empowers you to negotiate salary with poise and assertiveness. By recognizing and managing your own emotions, such as anxiety or self-doubt, you can approach the negotiation process with a clear mind and confident demeanor. Understanding the employer's priorities and constraints can help you make a compelling case for the salary you deserve, backed by research and evidence of your value to the company.

For example, a study by TalentSmart found that individuals with high emotional intelligence are more likely to succeed in job interviews and negotiations, as they can adapt to social situations, read nonverbal cues effectively, and express themselves authentically. (TalentSmart, 2023)

By leveraging emotional intelligence in the interview setting, you demonstrate your professionalism and confidence and showcase your ability to understand and connect with others, making you a standout candidate for the job.

Effective Emotional Communication

In any professional setting, the way we exchange ideas, give feedback, and manage conflicts can make or break the team's dynamics. EI injects a dose of *empathy* and clarity into these communications, ensuring that they build rather than bruise. (Salovey, 2006, 34-41)

But how do you go about fine-tuning your emotional communication skills? Start by practicing active listening. While the principle of active listening does not change depending on the environment or type of relationship, in the workplace, active listening might require an additional layer of *empathy*. For example, in a workplace setting, active listening can help you build stronger relationships with your colleagues, understand their perspectives better, and ultimately improve collaboration and productivity within the team. Imagine you are in a team meeting discussing a new project. By actively listening to your colleagues during the brainstorming session, you demonstrate that you value their input and ideas. As you listen attentively, you pick up on subtle cues about their enthusiasm, concerns, or areas of expertise. This shows respect for their contributions and helps you tailor your responses and suggestions to align with their thoughts and feelings.

Turning Adversaries into Allies

Think back to a time when you faced a standoff with a colleague. In such moments, a high EI can be your best ally. It equips you with the ability to navigate through conflicts by understanding what makes people tick and what ticks them off. In a team meeting, if a colleague expresses resistance to a proposed strategy, take the time to listen to their reasons and ask clarifying questions to uncover their underlying concerns. By showing understanding and adjusting the plan to address their key issues, you can transform their initial skepticism into enthusiastic support, fostering more effective collaboration and achieving better project outcomes. Acknowledging their concerns and proposing collaborative solutions that align with your goals can turn a potentially tense situation into a productive discussion that strengthens your working relationship. This skill helps in smoothing ruffled feathers and forging alliances that can propel your career to new heights.

Feedback and Growth: The EI Approach to Improvement

Giving and receiving feedback can sometimes be difficult but is essential for career development. It can feel like navigating a minefield blindfolded—step too far one way, and you might trigger an explosion of defensiveness; too far the other, and you risk the message getting lost in a cloud of softeners. But here's where EI comes into play. EI can help you transform feedback into constructive advice that benefits everyone involved.

When giving feedback with EI, the secret is *empathy* mixed with clarity. Start by framing your feedback to focus on behaviors and outcomes, not personality traits. For instance, instead of saying, "You're always so disorganized," try pinpointing an example, "I noticed that the last project was turned in past the deadline, which can disrupt the workflow. We could look at some strategies to help manage your project timelines better. This approach ensures that the feedback is less personal and more digestible but also opens up a pathway for constructive dialogue rather than a defensive shutdown.

Receiving feedback with EI, on the other hand, requires a thick skin but not a hard heart. You should listen actively, not just to respond but to understand. Resist the knee-jerk reaction to defend your turf, and instead, try to see feedback as a golden nugget of insight that could help polish your professional skills. When feedback comes your way, take a deep breath, park your emotions aside for a moment, and look for the core message. Is there a truth in there that could help you grow? By embracing feedback as a tool for self-improvement rather than a personal attack, you cultivate an environment where growth is part of the daily routine.

Achieving Career Success Through a Growth Mindset

Achieving career success hinges on the interplay between personal growth, emotional intelligence, and a growth mindset. These components form a dynamic trio that propels individuals towards professional excellence by fostering resilience, *self-awareness*, and continuous development.

A growth mindset catalyzes embracing challenges and reframing setbacks as opportunities for growth rather than obstacles. When coupled with EI, individuals can effectively manage feedback, setbacks, and personal development journeys with grace and insight, paving the way for enhanced performance and success in the workplace.

For instance, when confronted with a project setback, individuals with a growth mindset and strong EI skills do not succumb to defeatist attitudes. Instead, they leverage their emotional intelligence to regulate their responses, extract valuable lessons from the experience, and pivot toward improvement. By posing introspective queries like "What can I learn from this?" or "How can I approach this differently next time?", they transform setbacks into stepping stones for career growth and skill refinement.

Crafting a robust personal development plan becomes a strategic tool for aligning feedback with actionable goals aimed at professional enhancement. By honing in on emotional strengths, identifying areas for improvement, and setting SMART (specific, measurable, achievable, relevant, time-bound) goals, individuals can propel their career trajectories forward with purpose and intention. An example of a SMART goal could be, "I am going to secure a promotion to the next level within my current company by increasing my project management skills and taking on more leadership responsibilities within the next 12 months."

Celebrating milestones of personal growth and achievement, big or small, is pivotal in sustaining *motivation* and cultivating an emotionally intelligent workplace culture. Recognizing accomplishments, such as handling challenging feedback constructively or excelling under pressure, reinforces a growth mindset and nurtures a spirit of continuous improvement essential for career success.

Individuals can navigate challenges, seize opportunities, and cultivate meaningful professional relationships with *empathy*, clarity, and a steadfast commitment to ongoing learning and development by wielding personal growth and emotional intelligence as guiding beacons along their career paths. This holistic approach illuminates the pathway to career success and fulfillment, underpinned by the transformative power of personal growth and emotional intelligence.

In this chapter, we've navigated the intricacies of workplace communication and development through the lens of EI. From mastering effective emotional communication to securing that job or position using active listening techniques and a growth mindset, we've covered strategies that enhance professional relationships and build a foundation for a resilient, emotionally intelligent work environment. As we move forward, let's continue to apply these insights, fostering workplaces where *empathy* and understanding drive innovation and success. Next, we delve deeper into the role of EI in leadership, exploring how it shapes influential and inspiring leaders.

NINE

Emotional Intelligence & Leadership

Imagine walking into your office and instead of the usual buzz of stress and clattering keyboards, you're greeted with nods, smiles, and a palpable wave of positive vibes. It sounds like a fantasy workplace, right? The secret to turning this fantasy into reality isn't in lavish perks or over-the-top team-building exercises—it's all about weaving EI into the fabric of your daily interactions. This chapter is your blueprint for transforming your workplace with EI and enhancing your team's mood, productivity, and creativity. So, let's roll up our sleeves and dive into the art of emotional communication, navigating professional boundaries, and boosting team collaboration.

The Emotionally Intelligent Leader

An EI leader is akin to a skilled captain navigating through calm and stormy seas gracefully. These leaders possess a strong sense of *self-awareness* and *regulation*, have the profound ability to recognize, understand, and manage their own emotions, and they are equally adept at empathetically deciphering and influencing the emotional currents of others. (Goleman, 1995) But what does this look like in practice? Picture a leader who can sense tension in a team meeting, perhaps spotting a team member's subtle signs of discomfort. Instead of glossing over these cues, an EI-savvy leader addresses them directly, asking open-ended questions to draw out issues and concerns in a supportive manner. This approach alleviates immediate stress and fosters a culture where open communication is valued and encouraged. A study from the UK that surveyed the restaurant industry found that the performance of general managers depends on "their ability to be aware of and understand their own emotions."

Additionally, the study found that the profitability of their restaurants was highly dependent on two factors: social responsibility (i.e., managers' ability to identify with their place of work, the team within the outlet, its role in the local community and possibly the brand itself) and interpersonal relationships with the staff. (Langhorn, 2004, 220-230) Having high emotional intelligence is critical not just to employee satisfaction but also to the business's overall health.

The impact of such leadership stretches far beyond the confines of office walls. It leads to enhanced team morale, increased productivity, and a workplace that many dream of but few actually experience. This is because EI leaders prioritize relationships alongside results. They understand that the heart of their business lies not in numbers and charts but in the people driving those numbers. They are, put simply, masters at humanizing the workplace, transforming it into a space where employees feel genuinely valued and understood.

Influencing with Empathy

Empathetic leadership can turn routine team interactions into deeply engaging and motivating experiences. When leaders operate with *empathy*, they tune into the emotional frequencies of their team members. They become adept at understanding perspectives different from their own, which is crucial in a diverse workplace. For instance, when a project fails, an empathetic leader explores the emotional and practical reasons behind the failure without placing blame, setting the stage for learning instead of finger-pointing.

This approach helps resolve conflicts or challenges and celebrate successes. An empathetic leader acknowledges individual contributions in ways that resonate personally with each team member. For some, public recognition might be exhilarating; for others, a quiet thank-you note might hold more value. These nuanced acknowledgments boost morale and reinforce the value of all efforts, cultivating a profoundly committed and cohesive team.

Building Trust and Respect Through Empathy

Trust and respect are the bedrock of effective leadership, and here, too, EI plays a pivotal role. EI involves being consistently considerate and fair, cultivating an environment where trust and respect flourish. Leaders who show genuine, empathetic concern for their team's well-being and professional growth are rewarded with loyalty and high regard. This trust-building is about more than grand gestures; it's built through the everyday actions that show you care. An EI leader might remember a team member's upcoming challenging presentation and offer support or be approachable when issues arise.

Moreover, this trust extends to giving employees the autonomy to make decisions about their work. When leaders trust their teams to do their jobs well and support them rather than micromanage, it empowers individuals, enhances job satisfaction, and fosters a culture of mutual respect. This empowerment is a testament to the leader's confidence in their team, which in turn encourages employees to rise to the occasion.

Managing Emotions in Leadership

The ability to manage personal and team emotions often separates good leaders from great ones. EI leaders are adept at *self-regulation*, keeping their emotions in check, particularly in high-pressure situations. Consider a scenario where a key client unexpectedly terminates a long-standing contract with your company. While shock and disappointment are natural reactions, EI leaders manage their emotions effectively, setting a calm, controlled tone for their team. They navigate through such crises by staying focused, rallying their team, and deploying a clear plan of action. For this example, it would be imperative that the manager communicate transparently, remain cheerful and solution-oriented, and develop a recovery plan for this terminated contract. By effectively managing emotions and taking proactive steps to address the situation, EI leaders can navigate unexpected business challenges and guide their teams toward a successful recovery.

These leaders also empathize with and respond to their team's emotional needs. They can tell when to push for more effort and when to pull back and give the team a break, core components of *social skills* and "reading the room." By adjusting their leadership approach to their team's emotional state, they ensure that stress and burnout are minimized and productivity is maximized.

In leadership, as in life, EI isn't just an add-on; it's essential. It transforms leadership from merely exchanging commands and reports into a dynamic interplay of growth, *motivation*, and mutual respect. As leaders, nurturing your EI is one of the most profound ways to influence positively, build trust, and create a workplace that thrives and functions. Every interaction is an opportunity to practice and model EI, setting the tone for your team and shaping your organization's future.

Building Teams with Emotional Intelligence

Imagine you're at a family reunion. Some are tossing a football, others debate the merits of the latest political drama, and a few are trying to corral children excited on too much sugar. Despite the chaos, there's a harmony that underpins the gathering. Everyone knows their roles, understands each other's quirks, and, most importantly, values the collective family vibe. This scenario isn't too different from managing a team in the workplace, where EI acts much like the glue that holds a family reunion together—it ensures cohesion, understanding, and mutual respect, even when opinions clash, and stress levels rise.

The Foundation of Team Cohesion

Cohesion within a team doesn't magically appear. It's cultivated through shared experiences, mutual respect, and a deep understanding of each other's emotional landscapes. EI is critical here—it teaches us to look beyond the surface of what team members say or do to explore the why behind their actions. For instance, when a team member seems unusually quiet during a meeting, EI compels a leader to notice and care. Is the team member overworked? Are they feeling unheard? Addressing these concerns openly and with *empathy* not only resolves potential issues but also strengthens the trust and unity within the team.

This unity is further solidified when leaders use EI to foster an environment where team members feel safe to express their thoughts and feelings—a space where vulnerability is not seen as a weakness but as a courageous step towards genuine teamwork. By encouraging this level of openness, leaders set the tone for a cohesive team dynamic where each member feels valued and understood, paving the way for more harmonious and effective collaboration.

Team rituals can play a significant role. Regular check-ins, where team members can share updates and how they're feeling about their workload and the project, can prevent stress from building up and keep everyone aligned, which enhances team collaboration. Celebrating small wins and acknowledging individual contributions can boost morale and motivate the team.

Interactive Element: Team Emotional Intelligence Exercise

To put this into practice, try these quick team-building exercises in your next meeting:

- Emotional Check-In: Have each team member share one word describing how they feel about the project or their workload. This will foster emotional openness and also give insights into the team's morale and stress levels.

- Idea Validation: When discussing ideas, encourage each team member to contribute something positive about the concept before any critiques are offered. This ensures a balanced view and maintains a positive atmosphere. Addressing Emotional Challenges in Communication

By incorporating these exercises that promote emotional awareness and *empathy* into team meetings, a collaborative environment is nurtured, fostering trust, understanding, and effective communication among team members through emotional intelligence.

EI in Team Dynamics

Managing team dynamics with EI involves recognizing and valuing the diverse emotional strengths each team member brings to the table. It's about understanding that while one person may excel in high-pressure situations, another thrives in a calm, meticulously planned environment. Recognizing these differences and knowing how to leverage them underpins a team's success.

For instance, consider a project requiring innovative thinking and meticulous attention to detail. An emotionally intelligent leader with honed *social skills* assigns roles to each team member's emotional strengths—perhaps placing a highly creative team member in charge of brainstorming sessions while someone with a knack for detail handles project management aspects. This strategic allocation ensures that all aspects of the project are well-managed and contributes to personal satisfaction among team members, as each person feels their specific talents are being recognized and utilized effectively.

Moreover, EI is crucial in navigating the inevitable conflicts in any team setting. Instead of allowing disagreements to escalate into resentments, emotionally intelligent leaders use these situations as opportunities for growth and learning. They facilitate open discussions where different viewpoints are expressed and respected, guiding the team toward resolutions considering all perspectives. This effectively resolves the immediate conflict but also teaches team members valuable lessons in communication and compromise, reinforcing the team's ability to handle future challenges more effectively.

Navigating Workplace Conflicts

Understanding the emotional landscape of conflicts is crucial. Think of it this way: beneath every clash of opinions at work, there's a swirl of emotions—frustration, fear, or even misunderstanding. By tuning into these emotions, rather than just the surface arguments, you can address what's fueling the conflict.

Let's say a team member snaps at another during a meeting. It's easy to dismiss this as rudeness, but you can look deeper with EI. Perhaps that team member is stressed about an impending deadline or feeling undervalued. Recognizing these underlying feelings allows you to approach the conflict not as a battle to be won but as a problem to be understood and solved together. This perspective shift is essential because it moves the focus from blaming to understanding, setting the stage for genuine resolution.

Now, onto the art of de-escalation—a critical skill in your EI toolkit. The key here is to keep your cool when the office temperature rises. This means keeping your voice calm, body language open, and words focused on solutions rather than problems. Use phrases that validate others' feelings without necessarily agreeing with their point of view. For example, saying, "I see why that deadline felt unrealistic to you," acknowledges their feelings without compromising your position. It's like pouring water on the flames of conflict instead of fuel. Additionally, I suggest taking a brief pause if emotions run high. A short break can allow everyone to cool down, reflect, and return with a clearer head and a more cooperative attitude.

Building a culture of openness is your next strategy. This doesn't mean that everyone shares every thought or feeling all the time; instead, it's about creating an environment where people feel safe expressing their concerns or disagreements without fear of retaliation or ridicule. Start by leading by example. Be open about your challenges and how you're feeling about various projects. This openness can encourage others to do the same, promoting an atmosphere where conflicts are less likely to be swept under the rug and more likely to be addressed constructively. Regularly scheduled check-ins where team members can voice concerns or offer feedback can also help maintain this culture of openness. These sessions can act as a safety valve, releasing tensions before they escalate into conflicts.

Remember that every conflict holds a lesson. When approached with EI, conflicts can transform from stumbling blocks to stepping stones. Encourage your team to reflect on resolved conflicts. What triggered the disagreement? What worked (or didn't) in the resolution process? This reflection can provide valuable insights that strengthen your team's ability to handle future challenges. It's a bit like reviewing game tapes after a match; you refine your strategies for the next round by understanding your missteps and successes. By enhancing your EI, you become adept at de-escalating conflicts and transforming them into opportunities for team building and personal development.

Celebrating Team Successes

Nothing boosts a team's morale like celebrating its successes; doing so with EI can multiply the positive effects. Emotionally intelligent leaders recognize that the way success is celebrated can significantly impact the team's *motivation* and cohesion. They ensure that acknowledgements are inclusive, recognizing the contributions of every team member, from the intern who did the legwork to the senior staff who guided the project's strategy.

These celebrations are more than just pat-on-the-back moments; they reaffirm each team member's value to the group and remind them of the team's collective capability to achieve great things. Whether it's a shout-out at a team meeting, a company-wide email detailing the team's achievements, or an informal team outing to celebrate, these acts of recognition foster a strong sense of community and shared success.

Furthermore, emotionally intelligent leaders use these opportunities to connect celebrations with future goals. They highlight how the successes can be stepping stones to even more significant accomplishments. This approach maintains team *motivation* while planting a positive, forward-thinking mindset, ready to tackle whatever comes next with enthusiasm and a strong sense of unity.

Incorporating EI into team management transforms everyday teamwork into an extraordinary confluence of skills, talents, and emotional competencies. It ensures that teams work together and grow together, making each project not just a task to be completed but a journey of mutual development and shared victories. As we continue to explore the facets of emotional intelligence in leadership, remember that the heart of effective team management lies in achieving goals and nurturing the emotional bonds that make those achievements possible.

The Global Leader: EI Without Borders

In today's fast-paced, interconnected world, the role of a leader stretches across seas, cultures, and continents, making EI a global imperative. Imagine leading a team that spans different time zones, languages, and cultural backgrounds. EI becomes your passport, allowing you to navigate this diverse landscape with sensitivity and finesse. Leaders in such environments must manage the emotional and cultural nuances that influence team dynamics and productivity.

The globalization of business demands a shift from a local or regional mindset to a global one. This international mindset involves an openness to and awareness of diverse cultural, social, and economic landscapes. Global leaders must have the *motivation* to adapt to a global mindset to see the big picture and recognize the value of diverse perspectives in creating innovative solutions. For instance, while a strategy that works well in the U.S. might falter in Asia due to cultural differences in communication or decision-making, a leader with a global mindset understands these nuances and adapts strategies accordingly. This adaptability is rooted in a deep respect for diversity, an eagerness to learn from various cultural practices and viewpoints, and, most significantly, *empathy*.

Developing such a mindset starts with *self-awareness* and a genuine *motivation* to learn about the world and its many nuances. This includes understanding the historical, political, and social contexts that shape business practices and interpersonal interactions in different regions and the gaps in your knowledge. A global leader should be open to learning. For example, a leader might take the time to learn about the concept of 'face,' a critical social value in many Asian cultures, and consider how it affects business negotiations and team interactions in those contexts.

Moreover, effective global leadership relies heavily on specific EI skills such as cultural sensitivity and adaptability. Cultural sensitivity actively seeks to understand and respect different cultural norms and values. It means not imposing one's cultural standards but finding common ground where diverse perspectives can coexist and complement each other.

Leaders can engage in cross-cultural training, participate in international assignments, or collaborate in multicultural teams to cultivate these skills. These experiences improve cultural sensitivity and adaptability and help leaders build a repertoire of strategies for managing diverse teams effectively. For instance, role-playing exercises that simulate international business meetings can provide leaders with practical insights into how cultural differences influence interactions and how to navigate them successfully.

Another strategy for cultivating global EI is to foster a culture of inclusivity within the organization. This involves creating policies and practices that promote diversity in hiring, all business operations, team dynamics, and leadership. Inclusivity encourages open dialogue about cultural differences. A leader might provide platforms for sharing cultural insights and celebrating multicultural events. These initiatives enhance cultural understanding and demonstrate the organization's commitment to supporting a culturally diverse workforce.

In conclusion, as we wrap up this exploration of global leadership, remember that the essence of EI in a globalized world lies in embracing and celebrating diversity. *Empathy* and respect for all cultures are key in leadership. Now, let's turn our attention to the next chapter, where we will discover the true meaning of a quality life and how EI can support us in achieving it.

Section 4:

THE VALUE OF EMOTIONAL INTELLIGENCE

TEN

Emotional Intelligence & True Wealth

Picture this: You're standing at a crossroads, with success and growth on one side and a giant question mark on the other. You walk into a room buzzing with possibilities and realize that the key to unlocking your next big thing isn't just about cold, hard cash. It's about the richness of your life experiences, the wisdom you've gathered over the years, and the meaningful connections you've built with others. In this wild journey of high-stakes decisions, the treasure map lies in your bank account and your emotional toolbox. Welcome to the magical land where emotional intelligence meets the art of making it rain, where handling your feelings can steer your career and bring you personal joy.

Life Experience: The Jewel in the Crown of Emotional Intelligence

Life experience is like the glittering gem in the crown of emotional intelligence. It's what shapes the way we dance through life's twists and turns. With EI by our side, we can fully embrace every moment – sealing a significant deal, immersing ourselves in a new culture, or surviving a chaotic family reunion. EI boosts our *social skills*, strengthens our relationships, and propels us towards personal growth. Our trusty compass guides us through natural and symbolic jungles, sparking our curiosity, *empathy*, and inner strength. Mixing our life experiences with emotional intelligence creates a masterpiece of self-awareness, connection, and mind-blowing self-discovery that colors every inch of our lives.

Imagine you're off on a solo adventure to a place where even the birds speak a different language. It's normal to feel like a fish out of water, right? That's where EI swoops in to save the day, helping you wade through these alien experiences with wonder rather than panic. It nudges you to chat with the locals, stumble through a new phrase, and savor exotic dishes with an open heart. Each chat and taste becomes a brick in the grand mansion of your life experiences, expanding your view of the world and where you fit in it.

Now, let's bring that same spirit back home. You're at a family gathering where tensions can rival any international negotiation. But fear not; EI comes in handy here, too, nudging you to really listen to your folks, empathize with their stories, and respond with love. It helps you cherish these moments, seeing them as precious beads in the family necklace. Even when things get heated or opinions clash like bumper cars, your EI gives you the secret advantage to handle it all with empathy and strength. This deepens your bonds, creating memories filled with warmth and respect.

Regarding personal growth, EI is like a spotlight, turning everyday hurdles into golden learning opportunities. Think about a work project that's pushing all your buttons. Sure, stress is on the menu, but EI whispers in your ear to take a breather and dig into your emotional reactions. Why does that setback make you see red? What can your reactions teach you about your values, boundaries, and hot buttons? This introspection transforms a challenging situation into a crash course in *self-awareness* and toughness, leveling up your professional game and personal evolution.

But wait, there's more! EI isn't just about you – it's about how you sprinkle magic dust on everyone around you. It empowers you to be that ray of sunshine during dark times – a shoulder to lean on, a listening ear, or a cheerleader for your squad. EI's role extends beyond individual experiences to influence how you impact others. It empowers you to be the person who uplifts others during tough times—a supportive colleague, a compassionate friend, or a nurturing parent. You become the person who creates richer experiences for others, spinning a web of connections and kindness. This ripple effect of your EI doesn't just leave a trail of success and trophies; it weaves a legacy of deep relationships and positive vibes, echoing far into the future of your community and beyond.

Life Experience and the Art of Storytelling: Crafting Wisdom Through Emotional Intelligence

Your life is like a bestselling novel, with each adventure and emotion adding a new twist to the plot. You're the main character in a story filled with ups and downs, laughter and tears, victories and defeats. And guess what? You're also the storyteller, using your emotional intelligence to give meaning to these experiences and spin a unique tale.

Think of emotional intelligence as your trusty sidekick, helping you navigate through the crazy rollercoaster ride of life. It's like having a wise old friend whispering in your ear, nudging you to learn from your mistakes, celebrate your wins, and step out of your comfort zone occasionally.

Like a good book, a life worth living is about embracing challenges, seeking new adventures, and building deep connections with others. It's about collecting a treasure trove of experiences that shape you into the amazing person you're meant to be. It gives you plenty of material to reflect on as you grow wiser with age.

Research by McAdams (2013) shows that storytelling isn't just about sharing anecdotes; it's a fundamental part of who we are. By telling our stories with emotional intelligence, we gain a deeper understanding of ourselves and forge stronger bonds with those around us. It's like sprinkling a little magic dust on our life narrative, making it more prosperous, meaningful, and worth sharing with others.

As the years go by, our life experiences become like a treasure chest of wisdom, full of insights into resilience, love, and the beauty of human connections. Looking back on our past with emotional intelligence, we can distill these experiences into valuable life lessons that guide our actions and shape our future decisions.

Emotional intelligence is like an ace up the sleeve that accompanies you through all the twists and turns of life, whether exploring a new city or just chilling at home. It helps you savor each moment, learn from every experience, and positively impact the world around you in a truly authentic and fulfilling way.

So, let's raise a toast to a life well-lived, filled with diverse experiences and rich emotions, all woven together with the golden thread of emotional intelligence. Embrace each moment, cherish every memory, and tell your story with all the passion and depth it deserves. Because in the end, it's these stories that define us, inspire others, and light the way to wisdom and meaning in our journey through life. Cheers to that!

The Joys of Emotional Intelligence in Your Golden Years

It's very possible you used to be the fiery spark plug causing chaos at the office party. Still, now you're the calm, collected sage who's been through it all and can weather any storm with the grace of a seasoned sailor. It's not about burying your feelings—mastering them so they don't run the show; you do. This emotional finesse is like having gold in your back pocket as you age. It means fewer heart-pounding panic attacks and more heartwarming moments of zen. You can tackle life's curveballs—health scares, losing loved ones, or shifting social roles—with a resilience that comes from knowing you've got the emotional chops to handle it. It's not just talk either; studies show that older folks with high emotional intelligence often report better health, less stress, and an all-around better quality of life. (Shahini, 2023) It's like having an emotional gym membership you've used your whole life. Now you're reaping the benefits of all that emotional heavy lifting.

Now, let's talk about the legacy you're crafting. It's not just about the stuff you leave behind or the business deals you've sealed. It's about the lasting impact of the relationships you've nurtured and fortified with your emotional smarts. One of the most enduring legacies we can leave is the imprint we make on our kids and the generations to come. We create a legacy that transcends time by passing down values of kindness, *empathy*, and integrity through our actions and words. Research by Narvaez, Wang, Gleason,

Cheng, Lefever, and Deng (2013) suggests that positive parenting practices, such as emotional responsiveness and warmth, contribute to children's emotional well-being and moral development. By embodying these qualities and passing them on to our children, we shape a legacy of character and integrity for generations.

Another way we can leave a lasting mark is through acts of kindness and service that benefit our communities and the world at large. We can make a real difference by using our resources, time, and expertise to support causes that matter, whether it's education, healthcare, the environment, or social justice. These efforts create a legacy of impact and positive change that can uplift individuals and communities long after we're gone.

Let's not forget about the legacy we build through organizations and initiatives that aim to make the world a better place. By fostering a culture of collaboration, innovation, and social responsibility, we ensure that our contributions outlast us, leaving a legacy of collective progress and achievement that benefits society as a whole.

The legacies we leave through our relationships, values, philanthropy, and community impact are a testament to our emotional intelligence and connections with others. By nurturing these legacies with care and compassion, we ensure that our influence extends far beyond our lifetimes, shaping a kinder, more empathetic future for future generations. These relationships—with family, friends, and community members—accurately measure a life well-lived, reflecting the love, care, and understanding we've poured into them.

As this book has highlighted, EI is crucial in maintaining these relationships. It helps you navigate the complex dynamics of family life, friendships, and community interactions with a sensitivity that enriches your life and those around you. Your experiences and emotional insights give you a unique perspective that can offer valuable guidance and support to younger generations. By sharing your stories and lessons learned, you're passing on the wisdom of emotional intelligence—lessons in understanding, patience, forgiveness, and resilience—that will help them navigate their emotional journeys.

Think of this wisdom-sharing as your legacy in action, a priceless gift that shapes the character and choices of others. Imagine a world where these lessons become ingrained in the fabric of your family or community, enriching collective well-being. Emotional intelligence becomes more than a personal asset; it becomes a communal treasure, fostering understanding and connection among all. By leaving behind a legacy of emotional wisdom, you're ensuring that the world is a little kinder, more emotionally savvy, and more connected.

So, as you write the next chapter of your life story, take pride in knowing that your emotional intelligence is a gift that will keep giving, inspiring, and guiding others long after you've turned the final page.

The Hidden Goldmine: Emotional Intelligence in Self-Exploration

In the wild maze of emotional intelligence lies a treasure trove of riches that often goes unnoticed—the thrilling adventure of self-discovery. Beyond the flashy achievements and chatty relationships, there's a colorful tapestry of getting to know yourself, handling your inner chaos, and cultivating a profound *self-awareness*. This unexplored territory in emotional intelligence is like finding a secret stash that unlocks personal growth, resilience, and a hefty ol' dose of fulfillment that's way better than any shiny objects or social high-fives.

Embarking on the journey of self-discovery through the lens of emotional intelligence is like setting sail on a life-changing quest. It all starts with the guts to dive deep into your emotions, thoughts, and beliefs. You must peel away the layers of societal brainwashing, past goof-ups, and those self-imposed 'no-go' zones to reveal the real you. This process requires high emotional *self-awareness* and the ability to recognize and understand one's emotions, *motivations*, and triggers with clarity and objectivity. (Salovey & Mayer, 1990)

As you venture into your self-discovery journey, emotional intelligence becomes your trusty sidekick, shining a light into the dark corners of your mind and bringing to light parts of yourself hiding in the shadows. Through introspection, mindfulness, and self-reflection, you cultivate a deep sense of empathy and compassion towards yourself, fostering a nurturing inner dialogue characterized by kindness, acceptance, and non-judgment.

With emotional intelligence by your side, you're armed with the power to face your fears, doubts, and 'awkward dance moves' moments with guts and grit. It helps you navigate the stormy seas of self-doubt and confusion with style and poise, using your emotional tools to ride out life's roller coaster challenges. By developing a strong sense of emotional *self-regulation* and coping mechanisms, you cultivate the resilience to bounce back from setbacks and failures, viewing them as opportunities for growth and learning rather than insurmountable obstacles.

And there's more! Self-discovery through emotional intelligence opens up a sweet connection with your true, authentic self, letting you sync your actions, values, and dreams with your inner compass and purpose. By tuning into your emotional radar and tuning out the noise, you gain clarity and a roadmap to steer through life's twists and turns, heading towards paths that sing to your soul. This authentic alignment between your inner world and outer reality fosters a sense of integrity, authenticity, and wholeness that emanates from within and radiates outwards, influencing all aspects of your life. (Goleman, 1995)

The real treasure of self-discovery through emotional intelligence isn't in the gold stars or shiny toys but in the gift of truly knowing and embracing yourself, quirks and all. It's a journey of epic transformation and self-awakening, where the true you is unveiled, hugged, and celebrated with a big pat. So, as you keep exploring the wild world of emotional intelligence on your quest for self-discovery, may you find peace, wisdom, and a sense of freedom in the endless depths of your authentic self.

Relationships: The True Currency of Life

If you've ever had a cozy movie night on the couch and found yourself glued to the screen watching "It's a Wonderful Life," you'll remember that magical scene at the end where George Bailey realizes that the natural treasures of life aren't stashed in a bank vault, but are nestled in the warm embraces and heartfelt conversations with friends and family. This cinematic gem hits the nail on the head – the true riches we seek are the relationships we build along the way.

EI catalyzes friendship, marriage, business, and even one's relationship with oneself, transforming ordinary interactions into advantageous connections. Think about that lifelong buddy you can always count on. Sure, your shared history is the glue. Still, the mutual understanding, the unspoken nods of *empathy*, and the willingness to be there for each other without judgment keep the friendship flames burning bright.

Let's think about your spouse or partner. EI is the silent communicator, the peacekeeper, and sometimes, the spark that rekindles love when the daily grind dulls the romance. When tensions rise, as they often do in the closest relationships, your EI guides you to respond with compassion rather than frustration. You learn to navigate your needs and tackle problems in a way that builds bridges, not walls. It's all about finding that delicate balance where both of you feel heard, appreciated, and loved – and trust me, that kind of emotional dance is worth way more than any expensive gift.

And let's remember the professional realm! Here, EI serves as your strategic partner, helping you navigate complex networks of relationships with colleagues, clients, and stakeholders. EI supports you in cultivating trust and respect. By fostering a culture of support and camaraderie, you create a workplace where loyalty and enthusiasm flourish, boosting productivity and making your office where people actually want to be.

So, whether you're navigating the twists and turns of friendships, love, or office water cooler chats, remember—the true richness of life lies in the connections we nurture, the bonds we cherish, and the love we give and receive. In the grand scheme of things, that kind of wealth truly counts.

Family Bonds: Navigating the Treasures of Ever-Complicated Yet Rewarding Relationships

Picture this: your family is like a wacky sitcom, with each member playing a unique role in the dramedy of life. Through the ups and downs, the twists and turns, family bonds act as the glue that holds everything together, for better or worse.

Conger, Ge, Elder, and Lorenz's (1994) research highlights the significant impact of positive family dynamics on an individual's mental health and overall development. Positive family relationships, characterized by support, communication, and cohesion, have been shown to contribute to greater emotional resilience, self-esteem, and psychological well-being. When family members feel understood, valued, and connected, they are more likely to navigate life's challenges with confidence and adaptability.

Family dynamics mix love, chaos, growth, and forgiveness. From the battles over the TV remote to heart-to-heart talks with your grandma, every moment adds a layer to the epic saga of your family story.

Managing family relationships is like juggling flaming torches while riding a unicycle - it takes skill, patience, and a good sense of humor. Families build a legacy of love that lasts a lifetime by embracing each other's quirks, communicating openly, and creating unforgettable memories.

And let's remember the most important relationship of all - the one you have with yourself. It's like being your best friend, cheering yourself on through the highs and lows of life. This internal harmony is the most precious asset you can possess, for it paves the way for a fulfilled and balanced life.

Ultimately, it's not about how much stuff you have but the richness of the relationships you cherish. Like George Bailey in "It's a Wonderful Life," true wealth comes from the love we give and receive, the laughter we share, and the memories we create together. So, here's to embracing the beautiful messiness of family life and treasuring the priceless connections that make it all worthwhile.

A Chance for Your Story to Inspire Others

Sharing your successes as you hone your emotional intelligence will be a huge source of inspiration to others – and this is your chance!

Simply by sharing your honest opinion of this book, as well as something of your own story, you'll inspire new readers to get started on this transformative journey.

MAKE A LASTING IMPRESSION!

Thank you so much for your support. Those deep connections we've been talking about start here!

Scan the QR code below!

Conclusion

Throughout this book, we've explored how the core components of emotional intelligence—*self-awareness, self-regulation, motivation, empathy,* and *social skills*—interconnect to enhance every aspect of our lives. From nurturing relationships at home and fostering effective environments at work to guiding our children on their emotional journeys, EI is the thread that weaves through the fabric of all human interactions.

The power of EI to transform personal and professional lives cannot be overstated. Enhancing our EI opens doors to deeper relationships, more effective leadership, improved mental health, and expansive personal growth. Remember the strategies we've discussed: active listening, *empathy* exercises, stress management, and embracing technology like AI to further our emotional understanding. These tools are not just theoretical; they are practical steps that can lead to profound changes in how we relate to ourselves and others.

In this comprehensive exploration of EI, we have delved into the profound impact that *self-awareness, self-regulation, motivation, empathy,* and *social skills* can have on various aspects of our lives. From understanding the fundamental principles of EI to applying them in real-world scenarios, this journey has highlighted the transformative power of emotional intelligence.

By incorporating EI practices into personal relationships, parenting, cultural interactions, and even navigating the influence of technology, we have witnessed how EI serves as a guiding force in promoting harmony and understanding in diverse contexts. Moreover, in the workplace, EI emerges as a critical asset for career advancement and effective leadership, emphasizing the importance of emotional competence in professional success.

As we reflect on the value of emotional intelligence, it becomes evident that cultivating EI is not merely a theoretical concept but a practical approach to enhancing our overall well-being. Through active listening, *empathy* exercises, stress management techniques, and leveraging advancements like AI, we empower ourselves to foster deeper connections, lead with *empathy*, prioritize mental wellness, and embark on continuous personal development.

Ultimately, the lessons shared in this book underscore the significance of emotional intelligence in unlocking the true wealth of enriched relationships, fulfilling careers, and a harmonious inner world. By embracing and honing our emotional intelligence, we pave the way for a more compassionate, resilient, and rewarding personal and professional existence.

As you leave this book, I encourage you to pause and reflect on your EI journey. Recognize the growth you've already achieved and identify areas ripe for further development. Consider keeping a journal or diary as a companion in your quest for emotional mastery.

Please make a personal commitment today to prioritize your EI. Set specific, achievable goals and seek feedback from those you trust to help refine your path. Your commitment will ripple out, influencing your life and those around you.

Let's not stop here. Spread the word about the significance of EI. Share what you've learned and experienced. Advocate for EI in your communities and workplaces. Together, let's envision and work towards a world where EI is not an exceptional trait but a common language spoken by all.

Thank you for joining me on this transformative journey. Your engagement and dedication to enhancing your EI are commendable; they are acts of courage that contribute to a more compassionate, empathetic, and understanding world. Let's continue to support each other, sharing our successes and challenges as we strive towards a future where EI enriches every interaction. Together, we can create a legacy of emotional wisdom to enhance future generations.

Here's to our continued journey toward an emotionally intelligent life filled with deep connections and meaningful experiences. Thank you, indeed, for being a vital part of this adventure.

References

- Audrin, C., & Audrin, B. (2023, May 2). More than just emotional intelligence online: introducing "digital emotional intelligence." Frontiers in Psychology. https://doi.org/10.3389/fpsyg.2023.1154355
- Brackett, M. A., & Katulak, N. A. (2006). Emotional Intelligence in the Classroom: Skill-Based Training for Teachers and Students. In J. Ciarrochi, J. P. Forgas, & J. D. Mayer (Eds.), Emotional Intelligence in Everyday Life: A Scientific Inquiry (pp. 172–188). Psychology Press.
- Brackett, M. A., & Rivers, S. E. (2014). Transformative School Leadership and Emotional Intelligence: A Developmental Study. Educational Management Administration & Leadership, 42(2), 120–138.
- Brackett, M. A., & Salovey, P. (2006). Measuring emotional intelligence with the Mayer-Salovey-Caruso Emotional Intelligence Test (MSCEIT). In K. R. Scherer, R. R. Behnke, & T. B. Cohn (Eds.), *The handbook of emotional intelligence* (pp. 267-288). Wiley.
- Brackett, M. A. (2014). Emotional intelligence: Key readings on the Mayer and Salovey model. Society for Industrial and Organizational Psychology.
- Crawford, D. W., Houts, R. M., Huston, T. L., & George, L. J. (2002). Compatibility, leisure, and satisfaction in marital relationships. Journal of Marriage and Family, 64(2), 433-449.
- Conger, R. D., Ge, X., Elder, G. H., & Lorenz, F. O. (1994). Economic stress, coercive family process, and developmental problems of adolescents. *Child Development, 65*(2), 541-561.
- Decety, J., & Cowell, J. M. (2018). The Complex Relation Between Morality and Empathy. Trends in Cognitive Sciences, 22(6), 531–533.
- Denham, S. A., Bassett, H. H., & Zinsser, K. (2012). Early Childhood Teachers as Socializers of Young Children's Emotional Competence. Early Childhood Education Journal, 40(3), 137–143.

- Goleman, D. (1995). Emotional Intelligence: Why It Can Matter More Than IQ. Bantam Books.
- Goleman, D., Boyatzis, R., & McKee, A. (2002). Primal leadership: Realizing the power of emotional intelligence. Harvard Business Press.
- Goleman, D. (1995). *Emotional intelligence: Why it can matter more than IQ*. Bantam Books.
- Gottman, J. M. (2016). *The seven principles for making marriage work: A practical guide from the country's foremost relationship expert*. Harmony.
- Gottman, J. M., & Silver, N. (2016). The Seven Principles for Making Marriage Work: A Practical Guide from the Country's Foremost Relationship Expert. Harmony.
- Gtd. (2023, October 18). Why focus on emotional intelligence? learn why here. TalentSmartEQ. https://www.talentsmarteq.com/emotional-intelligence-can-boost-your-career-and-save-your-life/
- Hoffman, H. G., & Patterson, D. R. (2017). Virtual reality therapy. In B. O. O'Donohue & L. Fisher (Eds.), Cognitive behavior therapy: Core principles for practice (pp. 311-328). Wiley.
- Hoffman, L., Mar, R. A., & Mogilner, C. (2017). Aging and wisdom: Culture matters. *The Journals of Gerontology: Series B, 72*(6), 958-968.
- Jordan, P. J., Ashkanasy, N. M., Härtel, C. E., & Hooper, G. S. (2002). Workgroup emotional intelligence: Scale development and relationship to team process effectiveness and goal focus. Human Resource Management Review, 12(2), 195-214.
- Langhorn, S. (2004, June 1). How emotional intelligence can improve management performance. International Journal of Contemporary Hospitality Management, 16(4), 220–230. https://doi.org/10.1108/09596110410537379
- Lopes, P. N., Brackett, M. A., Nezlek, J. B., Schütz, A., Sellin, I., & Salovey, P. (2004). Emotional Intelligence and Social Interaction. Personality and Social Psychology Bulletin, 30(8), 1018–1034.
- Matsumoto, D., & Hwang, H. S. (2018). Culture and Emotion: The Integration of Biological and Cultural Contributions. Journal of Cross-Cultural Psychology
- McAdams, D. P. (2013). The psychological self as actor, agent, and author. *Perspectives on Psychological Science, 8*(3), 272-295.

- Narvaez, D., Wang, L., Gleason, T. R., Cheng, A., Lefever, J. B., & Deng, L. (2013). The importance of early bonding on the long-term mental health and resilience of children. *Psychology, 4*(06), 441-447.
- Shahini, M., & Pakenham, K. I. (2023). Emotional intelligence and quality of life in older adults: The mediating role of psychological distress. **Aging & Mental Health**, 27(3), 374-383.
- "30 Best Quotes About Emotional Intelligence." ThinkPsych. Last modified February 2, 2023. https://thinkpsych.com/blogs/posts/30-best-quotes-about-emotional-intelligence.

Printed in Great Britain
by Amazon